WELCOME TO COLORING: SUPPLIES

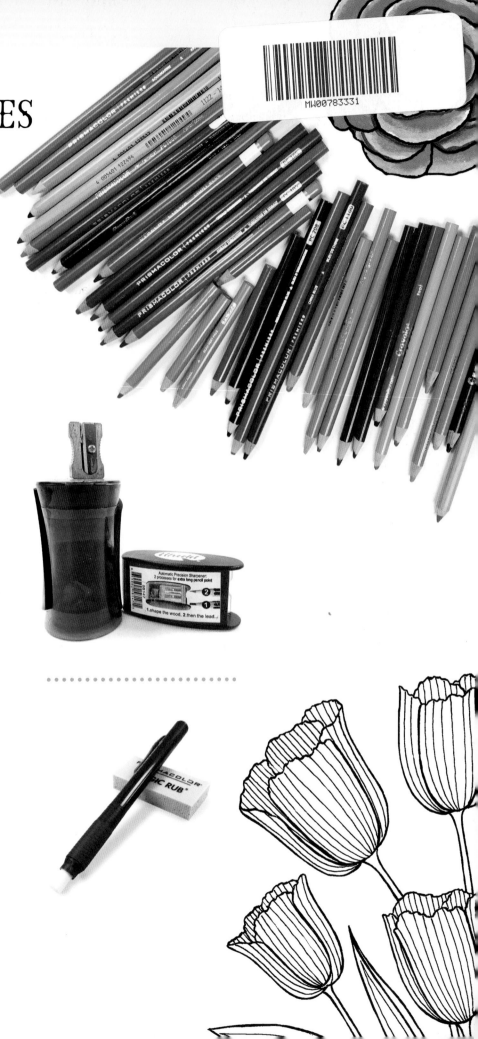

You can use any medium to color the designs in this book—markers, colored pencils, pens, gel pens, etc. It's all about what YOU love to use! Have fun experimenting with different mediums and brands. My favorite coloring supplies are colored pencils, pencil sharpeners, and erasers.

Colored pencils. I like to use pencils with both hard and soft leads. Pencils with soft leads are great for filling in large areas and blending. Pencils with hard leads achieve crisp, clean lines, making them excellent for detail work and filling in small spaces. Over the years, I have collected a variety of colored pencil brands. I encourage you to experiment with different brands until you find one (or more!) that you really love to work with. I keep my pencils separated into color groups. This allows me to quickly see the range of light and dark shades I have for each color.

Pencil sharpeners. Because I love working with colored pencils, I need a great pencil sharpener. Just like with my pencils, I use more than one type of pencil sharpener depending on the type of point I want to have. I use different points on my pencils depending on the effect I'm trying to create. If you are just starting out, find a sharpener that will give your pencil a strong, sharp point. If you discover you love working with colored pencils as much as I do, you might want to experiment with a few different sharpeners to create different points. Remember that pencils with softer leads are more difficult to sharpen to a fine point than their hard lead counterparts, so be patient!

Erasers. These are helpful for correcting mistakes and smudges or for adding highlights by lifting off some of the color. I like to use a pencil-style eraser that works like a mechanical pencil, allowing me to "click" out more of the eraser as I need it. For big spaces, I use a more traditional block eraser.

CREATIVE PROCESS: HOW MY ART BECOMES A COLORING PAGE

My creative process can start with anything from a phrase or a word to a feeling or an image! I focus on that inspiration and use it to develop a rough sketch. The sketch allows me to decide how I want to put the word or image and the rest of the artwork together.

Sometimes, a sketch inspires me to create another piece of art, like a mixed-media painting! If you are inspired by one of these coloring pages, don't be afraid to take it out of the book! Frame your art, decoupage it onto a canvas or wood surface, or use it for another craft project.

If I'm planning to turn the design into a coloring page, I redraw it in ink and add patterning. I designed fabric for years, which has given me lots of patterns to use in my coloring designs!

Once I am happy with the ink design and patterning, I import it to my computer as a digital image. Through the magic of my computer and design software, I'm able to turn the design into chalkboard art by adding a black chalkboard background and changing some of the black lines to white.

Once I've finalized the design on the computer, the real fun begins... I get to start coloring! For "Dream Big!", I knew I wanted a limited color palette using mostly cool colors and only a few warm colors to add some pop. When I'm finished coloring, I get to share my design with you!

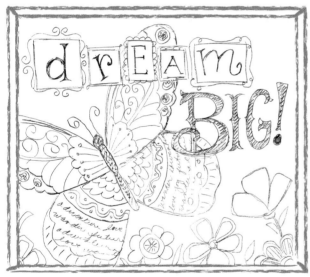

Every design starts out as a rough pencil sketch that can be inspired by almost anything!

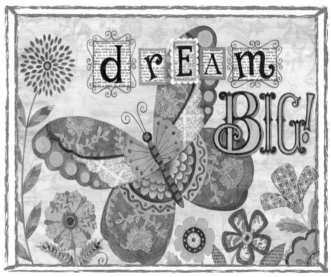

Sometimes a design needs to come off the page and transform into something else, like this mixed-media painting. If inspiration grabs you, follow it!

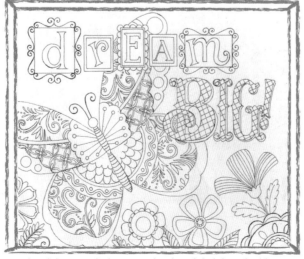

To turn a sketch into a coloring page, I redraw it in ink and add patterning. I take lots of inspiration from my years as a fabric designer.

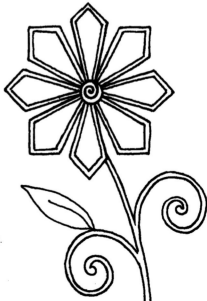

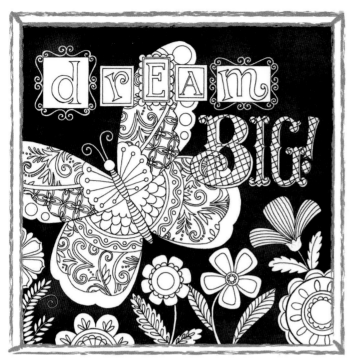

When the design is ready, it's imported to the computer and turned into chalkboard art through the addition of a chalky black background.

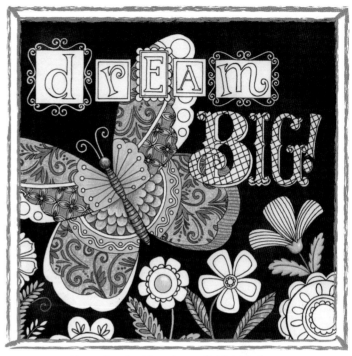

I love when I get to color my finished design.

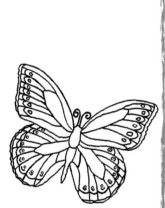

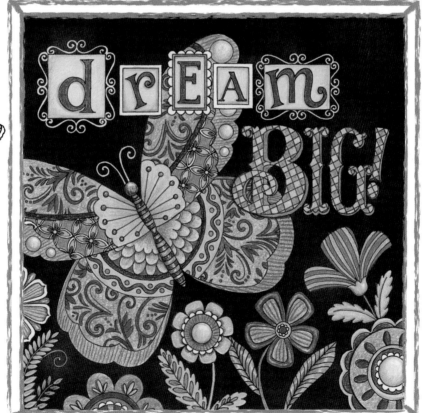

And I love sharing the finished product with you!

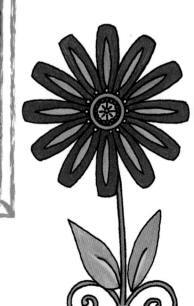

HERE ARE SOME
MORE EXAMPLES OF ART
(CHALKBOARD AND MORE!)
THAT I HAVE CREATED!

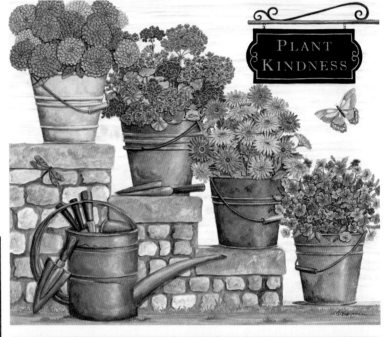

PLANT KINDNESS

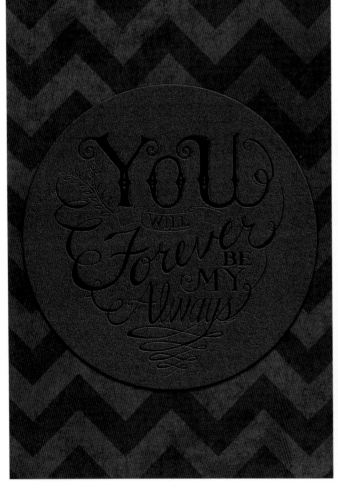

You WILL Forever BE MY Always

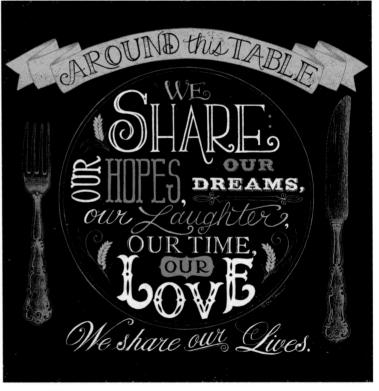

AROUND this TABLE
WE SHARE:
OUR HOPES, OUR DREAMS,
our Laughter,
OUR TIME,
OUR LOVE
We share our Lives.

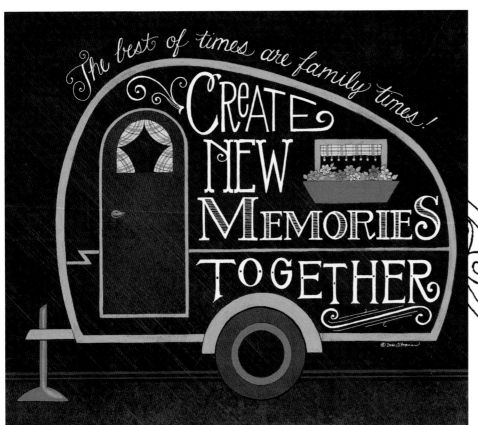

The best of times are family times!

CREATE
NEW
MEMORIES
TOGETHER

© Deb Strain

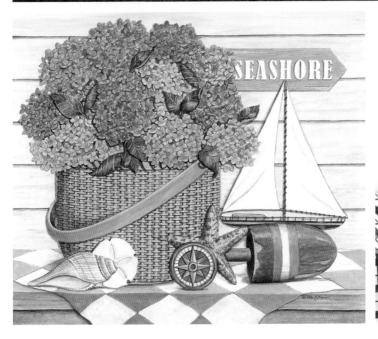

SEASHORE

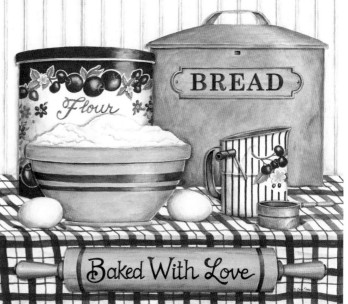

Flour

BREAD

Baked With Love

COLOR THEORY

Picking the colors you want to use for a design can be intimidating, but it doesn't have to be! Some basic understanding of color theory will go a long way toward making you feel more comfortable about choosing colors. Ultimately, though, it's good to remember that there is no right way or wrong way to color a design in this book, so don't be afraid to dive in!

It all starts with the primary colors red, yellow, and blue. These three colors can be mixed to create a whole rainbow, but they cannot be created by mixing other colors—this is why they are "primary." If you mix two primary colors, you will get the secondary colors orange (red + yellow), green (yellow + blue), and purple (blue + red). Mixing a primary color and a secondary color will result in a tertiary color. These include orange-yellow, yellow-green, green-blue, blue-purple, red-purple, and orange-red. Any primary, secondary, or tertiary color can be darkened or

lightened by the addition of white or black. The result is a tint or shade of the original color. For example, pink is a tint of red created by adding white, and burgundy is a shade of red created by adding black.

Take a look at the color wheel. It is your most helpful tool when it comes to understanding how colors relate to one another. Think of the color wheel as having two sides. On one side are the warm colors yellow, orange, and red. On the other side are the cool colors green, blue, and purple. Warm colors are bold and invoke excitement. They will pop out of your design, especially when paired with cool colors. Cool colors are calm and invoke relaxation and peacefulness. They will recede in a design. Warm colors will always pair well with one another and cool colors will always pair well with one another.

Another handy color relationship you should be aware of is analogous colors. Analogous colors are next to

one another on the color wheel. One reason warm colors and cool colors go well together is because they are analogous, but you don't have to limit yourself to warm and cool colors only. A mix of warm and cool analogous colors will make a great color scheme. For example, blue and green (both cool) pair well with yellow (warm).

One final color relationship for your arsenal is complementary colors. Complementary colors are directly opposite one another on the color wheel. If you look at the color wheel, you'll see that all complementary pairings contain a warm and a cool color. For example, orange (warm) and blue (cool). As their name suggests, complementary colors "complement" one another. They also stand out against one another more than they do against any other color. You can use this relationship to create some real impact!

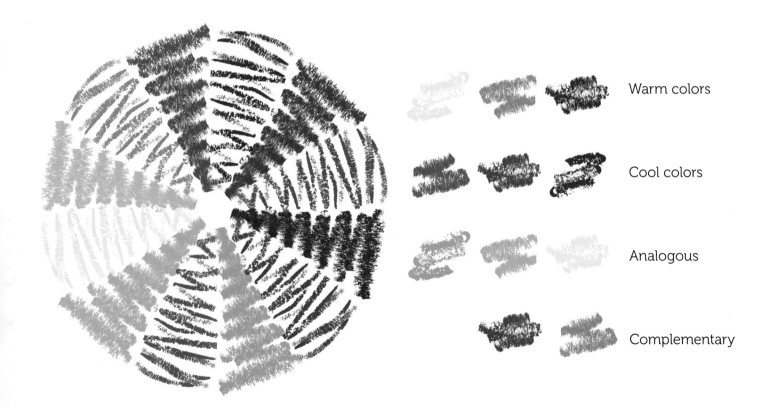

Warm colors

Cool colors

Analogous

Complementary

TIPS AND TRICKS FOR CHALKBOARD ART

The black chalkboard background used for these pieces adds another element to consider when coloring. Here are some tips and tricks that you might find helpful.

Use strong colors. This doesn't necessarily mean that you need to use bright colors, just ones with strong saturation (that don't look washed out). You may have to apply two or three layers of a color to create a rich, strong appearance. You'll want your colors to have this intensity so they stand out against the black chalkboard background, making the colored area the focal point rather than the chalkboard.

Plan ahead. Think about the colors you'd like to use before you start coloring. You might want to use colors from one color family. For example, blues, teals, purples, and greens (cool colors). Areas colored with cool colors tend to recede. To make areas pop or stand out, accent them with a color from another color family. For example yellows or oranges (warm colors) will stand out against your blue, purple, and green cool colors. Using colors primarily from one color group with only accents from another group will give your finished piece a cohesive appearance. If you want a fun, vibrant look—go crazy! Use colors from a variety of color families.

Black and white are colors, too! Because you are working on a black background, white will stand out against it the most. If you want a certain area to stand out, or if you are worried about a particularly fine detail getting lost, leave them white. For example, I left the fine antennae of the butterfly white, as well as some of the borders around the letters in "dream."

Leave some lines. You can also use the black lines that are already part of the design to add to your patterns and create definition. Leaving some black showing within colored areas helps tie in or balance the black background.

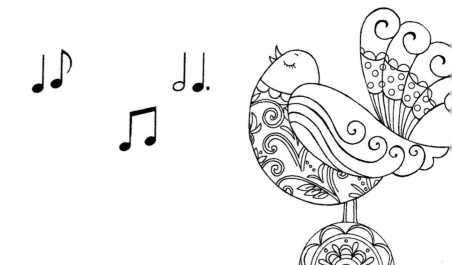

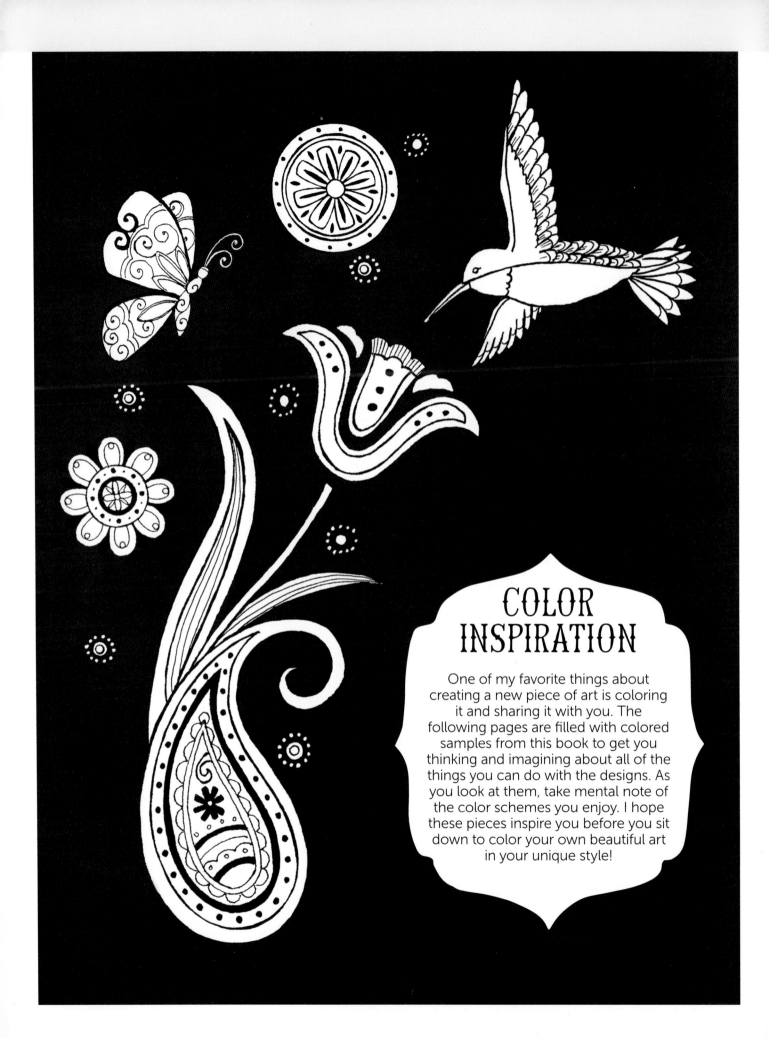

COLOR INSPIRATION

One of my favorite things about creating a new piece of art is coloring it and sharing it with you. The following pages are filled with colored samples from this book to get you thinking and imagining about all of the things you can do with the designs. As you look at them, take mental note of the color schemes you enjoy. I hope these pieces inspire you before you sit down to color your own beautiful art in your unique style!

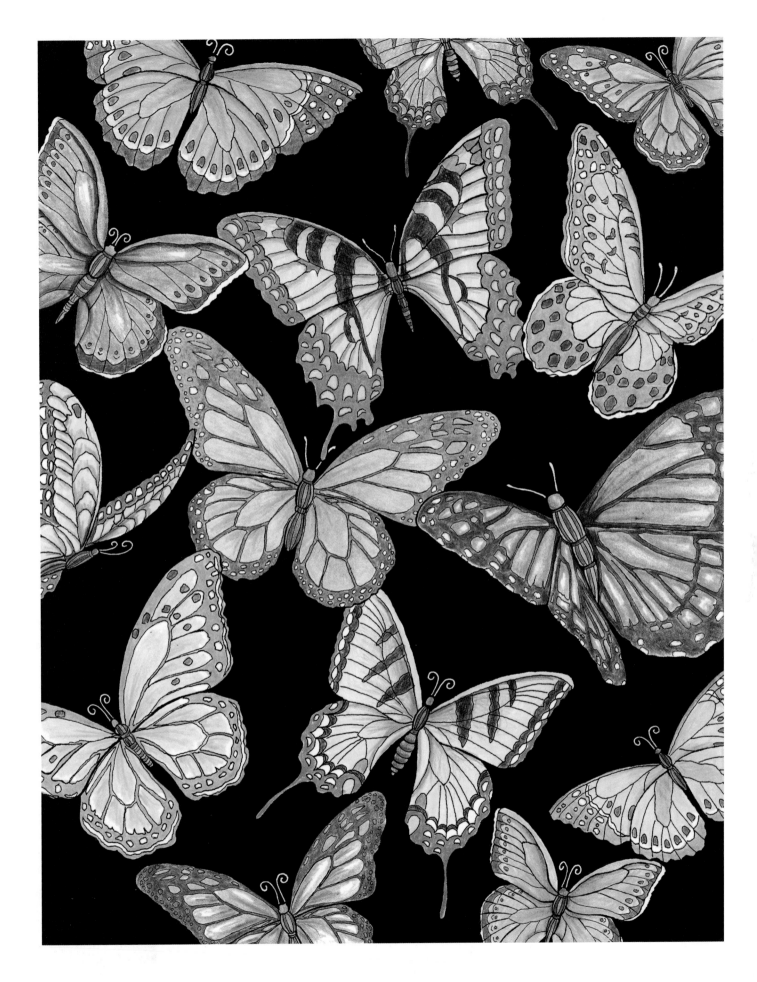

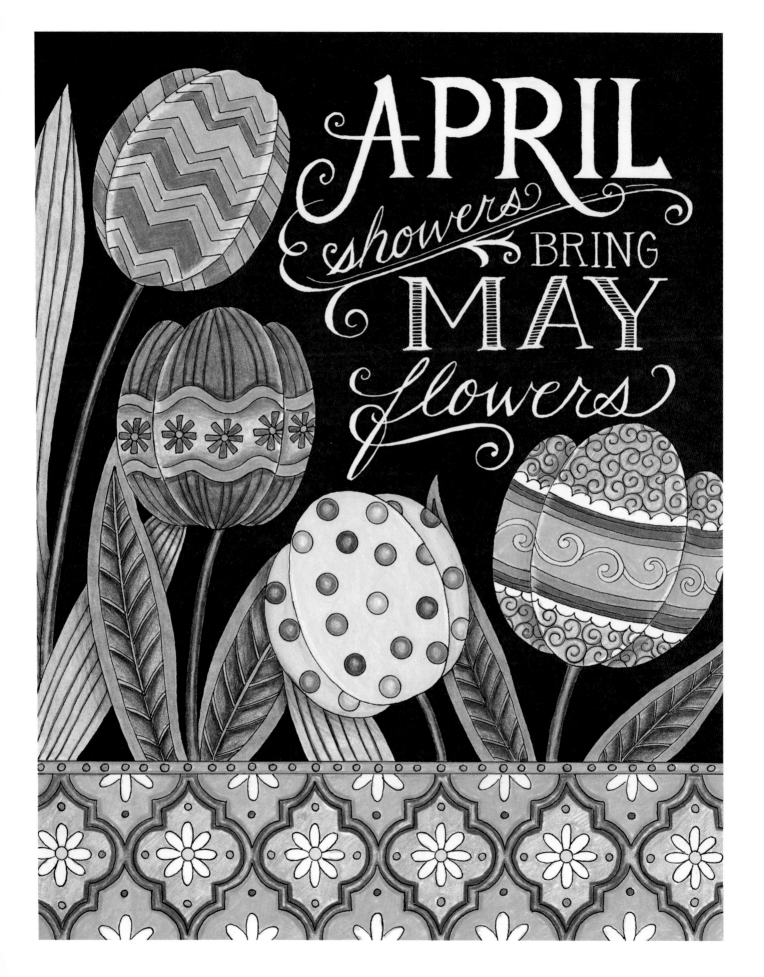

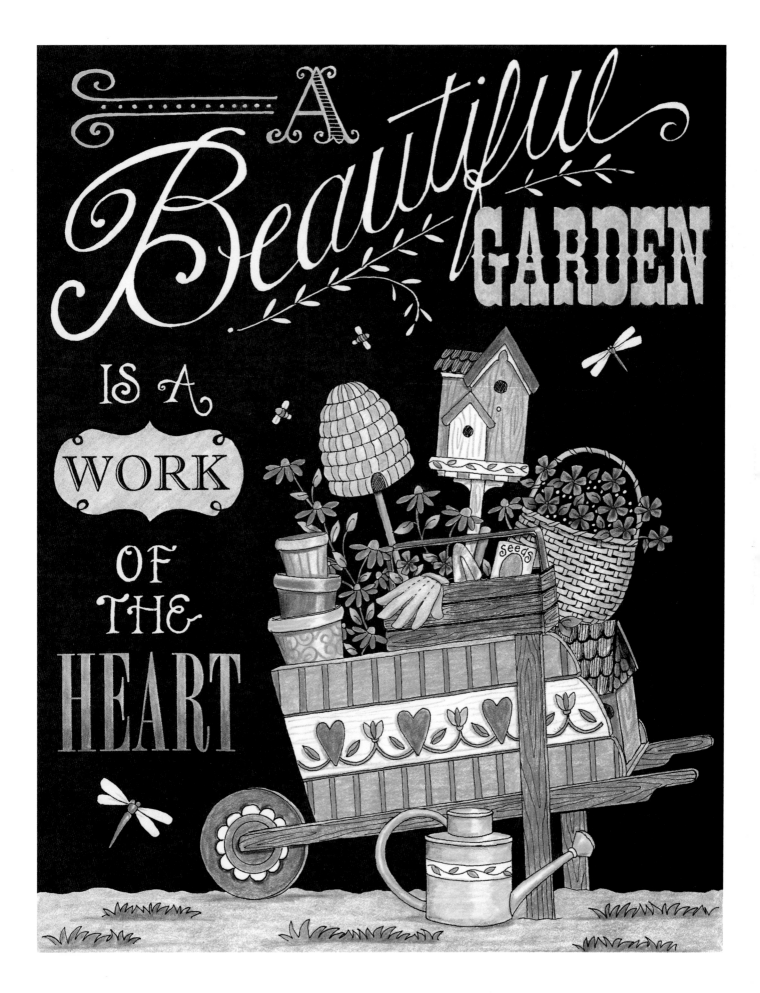

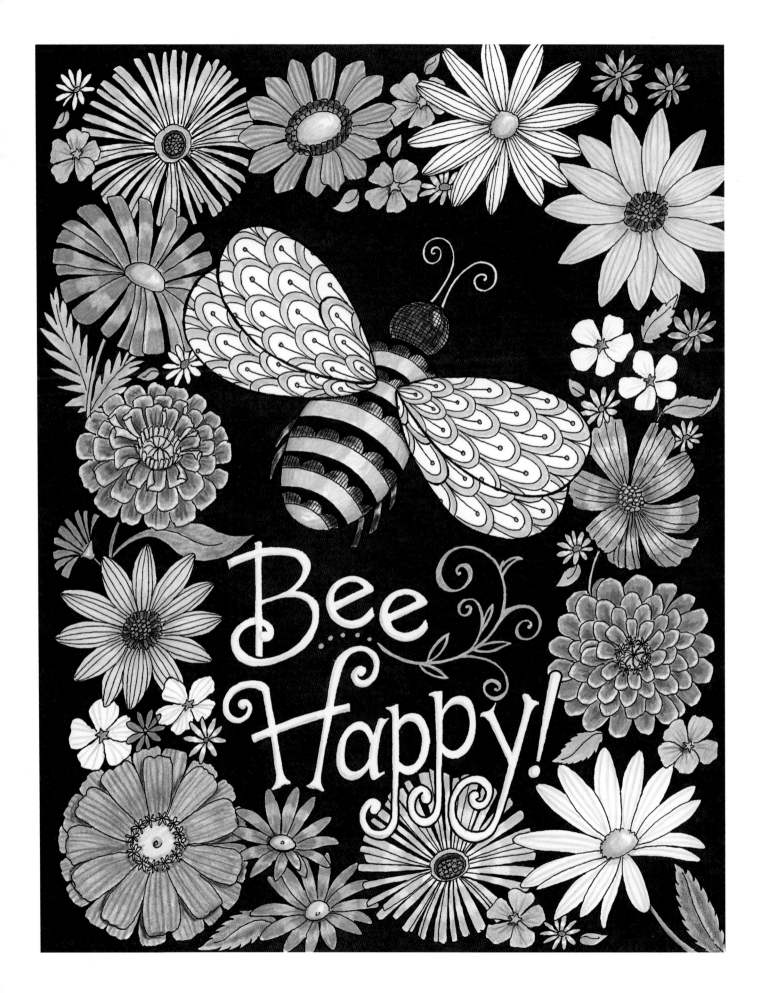

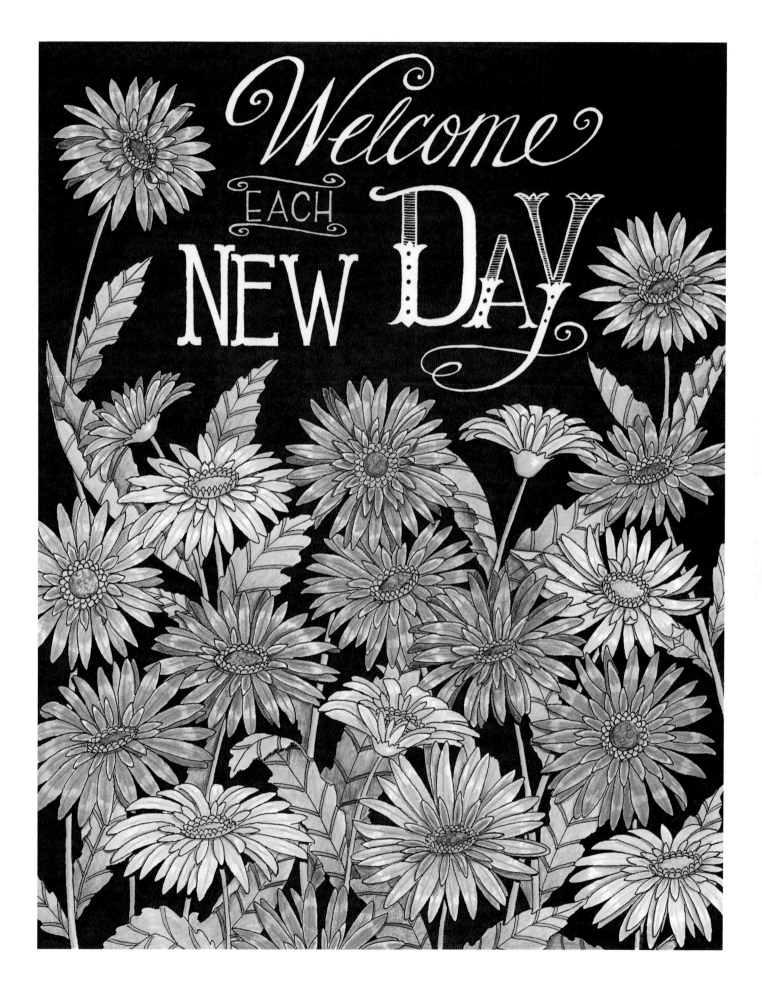

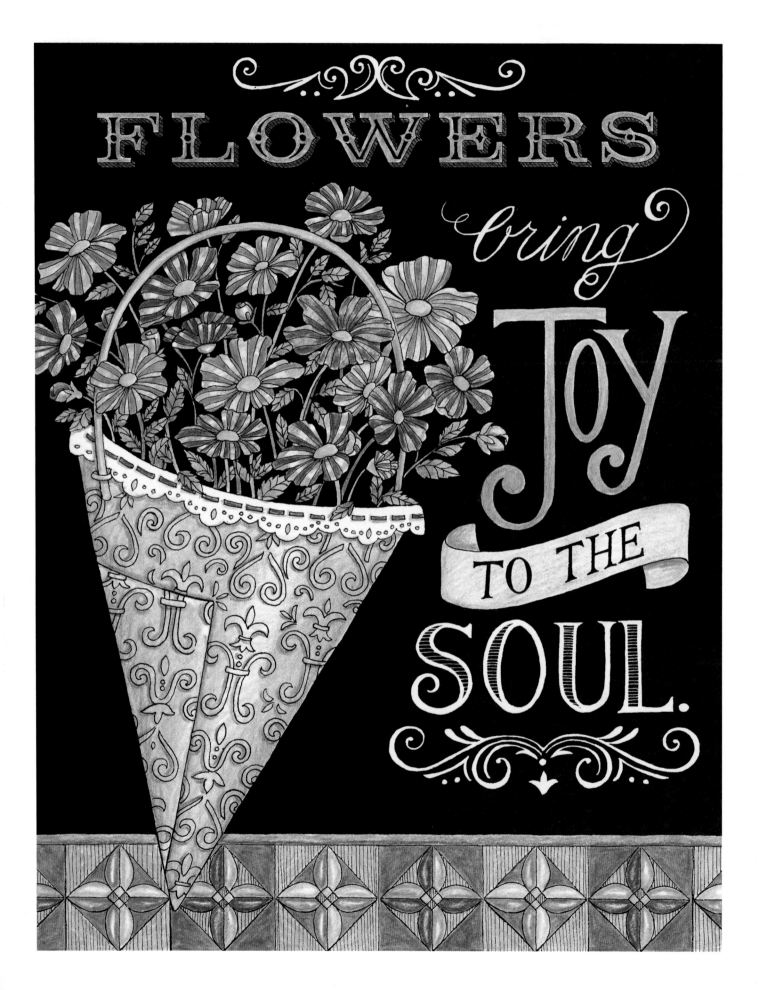

FLOWERS bring JOY TO THE SOUL.

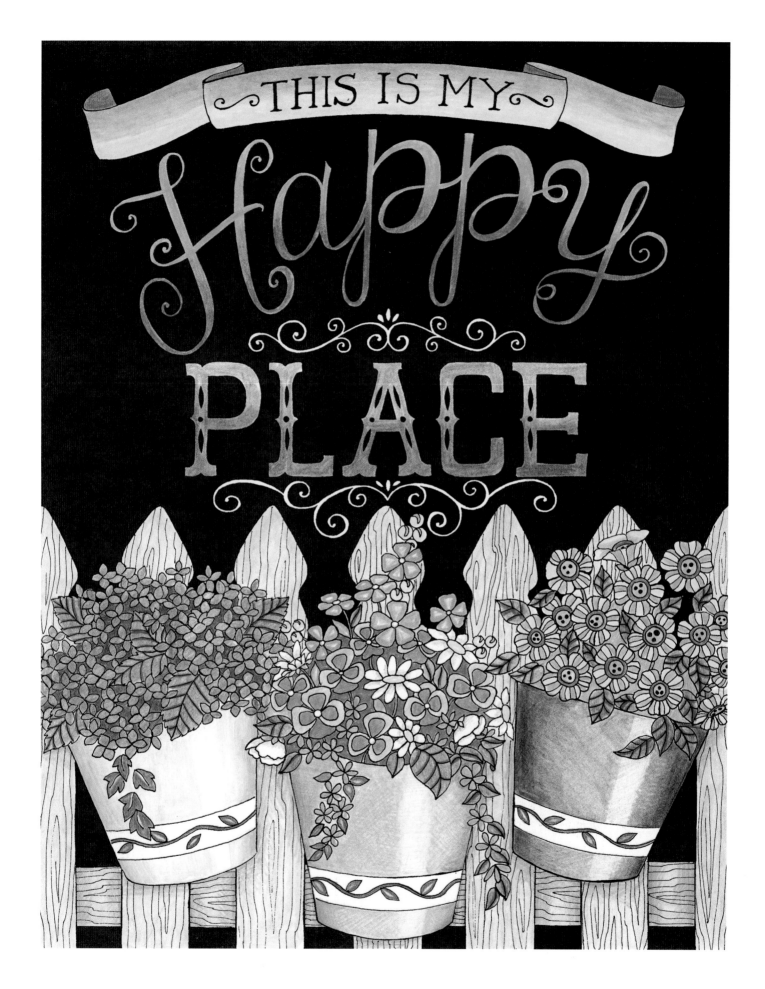

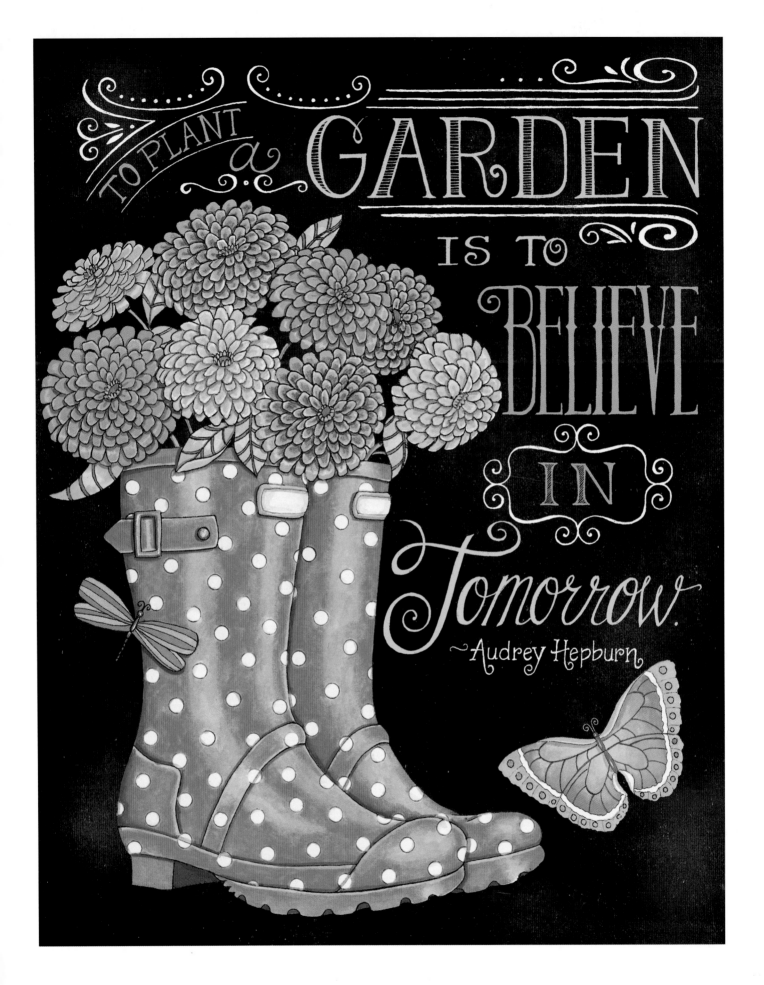

TO PLANT a GARDEN IS TO BELIEVE IN Tomorrow.
~Audrey Hepburn

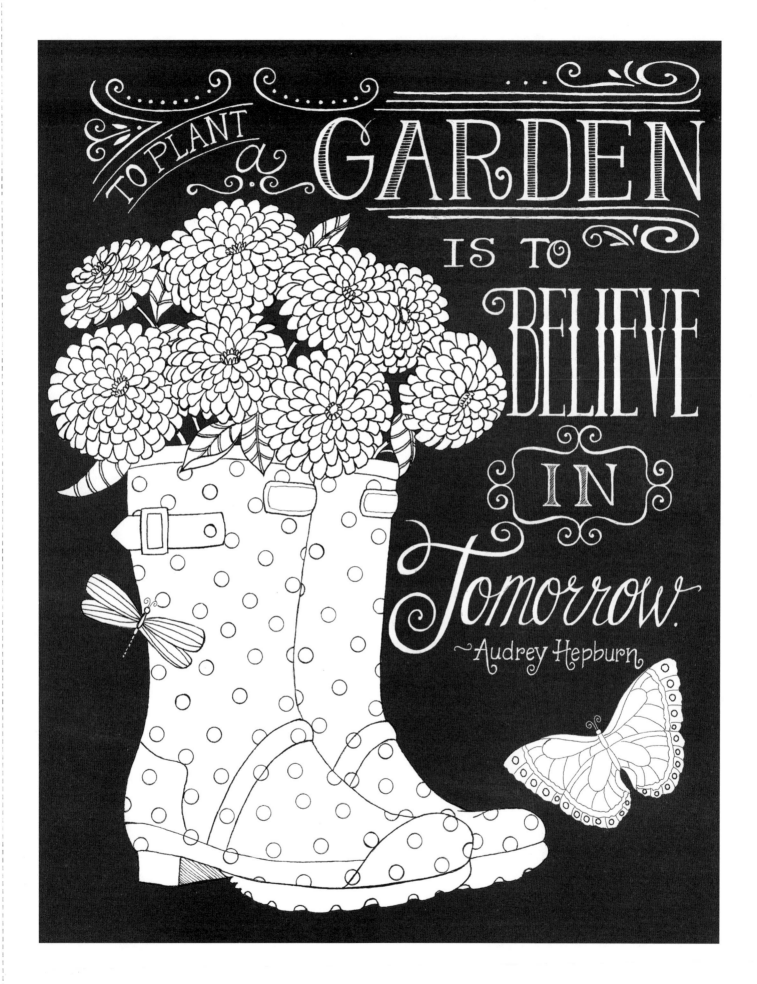

TO PLANT a GARDEN IS TO BELIEVE IN Tomorrow.
~Audrey Hepburn

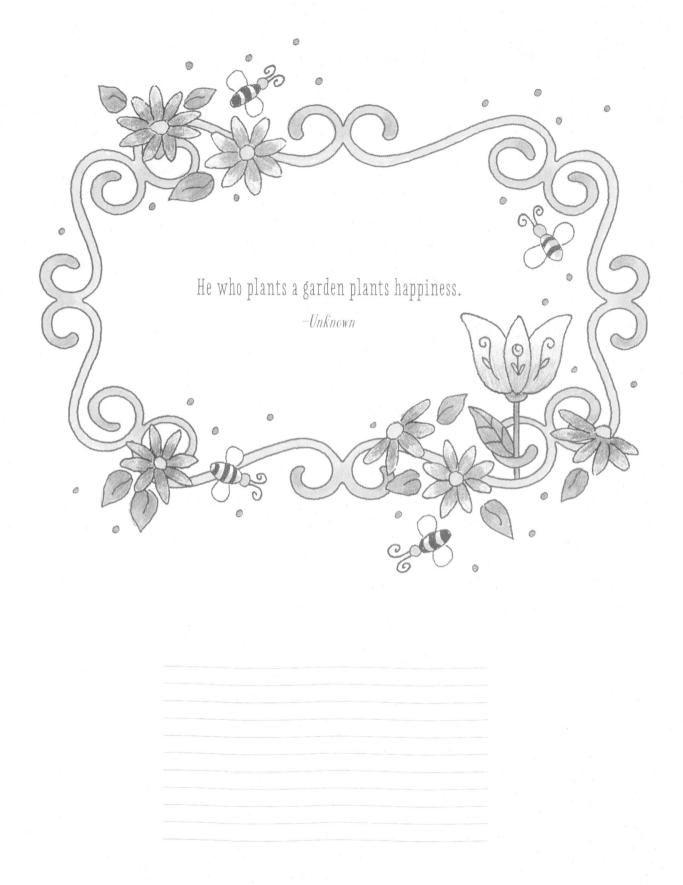

He who plants a garden plants happiness.

–Unknown

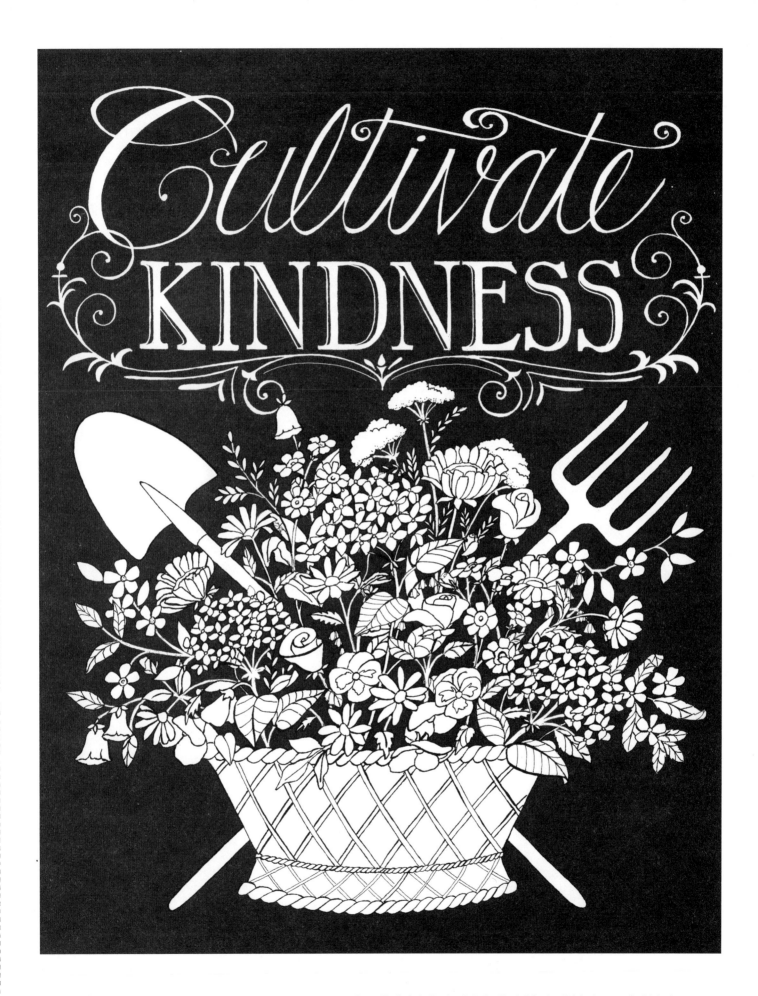

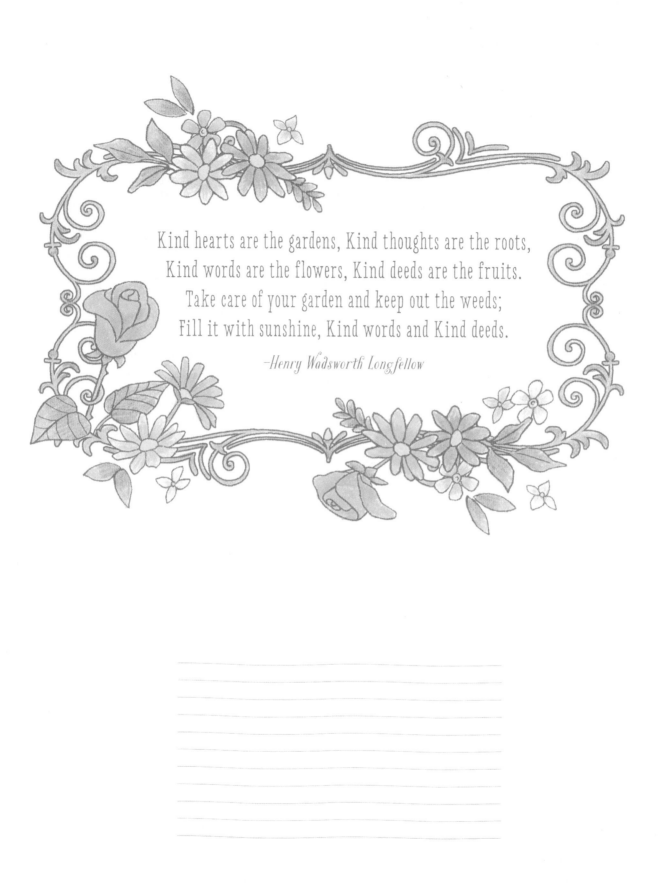

Kind hearts are the gardens, Kind thoughts are the roots,
Kind words are the flowers, Kind deeds are the fruits.
Take care of your garden and keep out the weeds;
Fill it with sunshine, Kind words and Kind deeds.

—Henry Wadsworth Longfellow

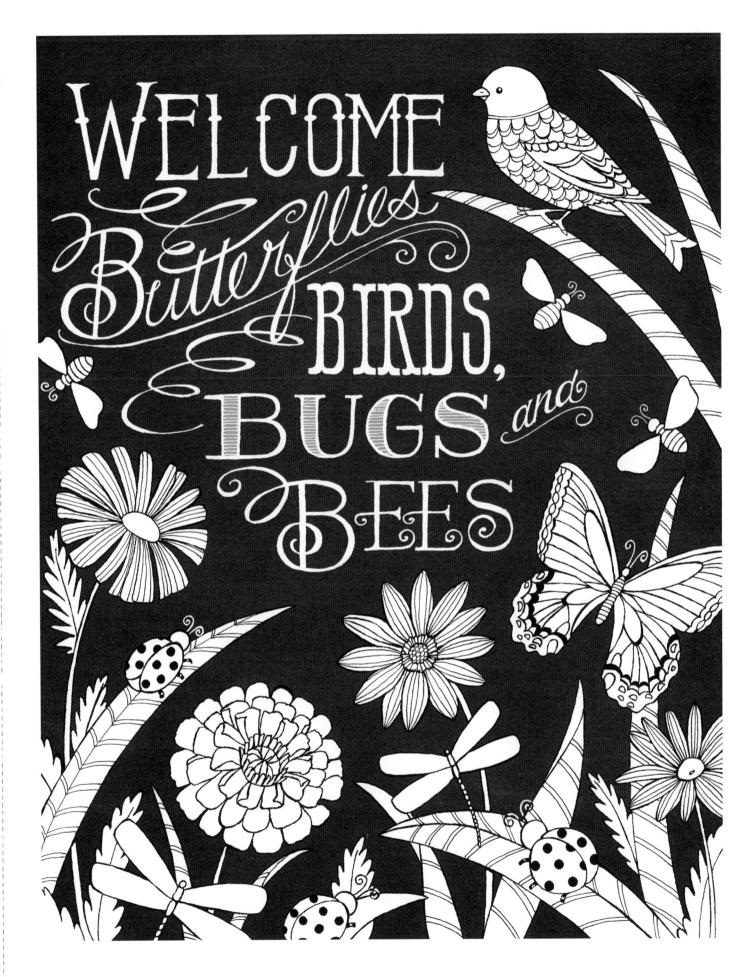

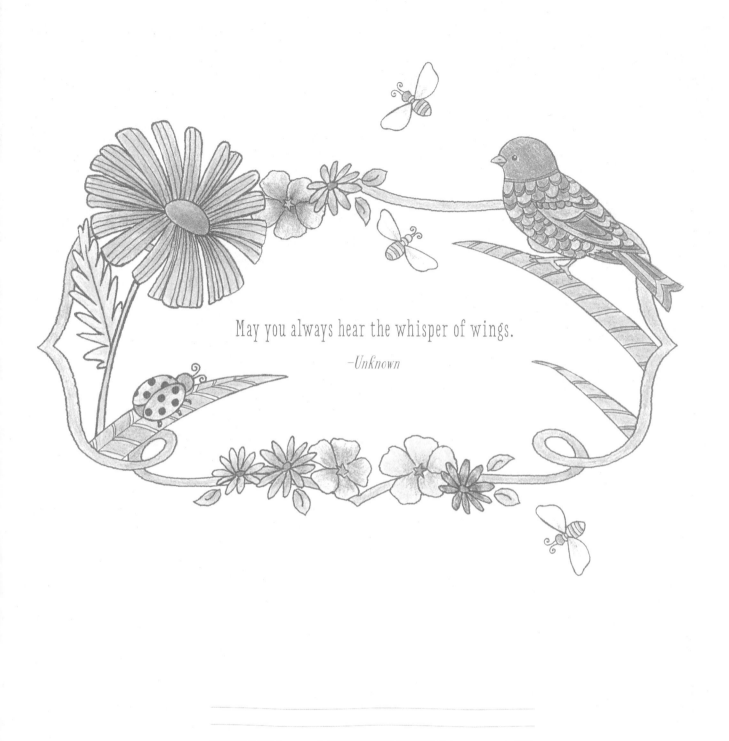

May you always hear the whisper of wings.

–Unknown

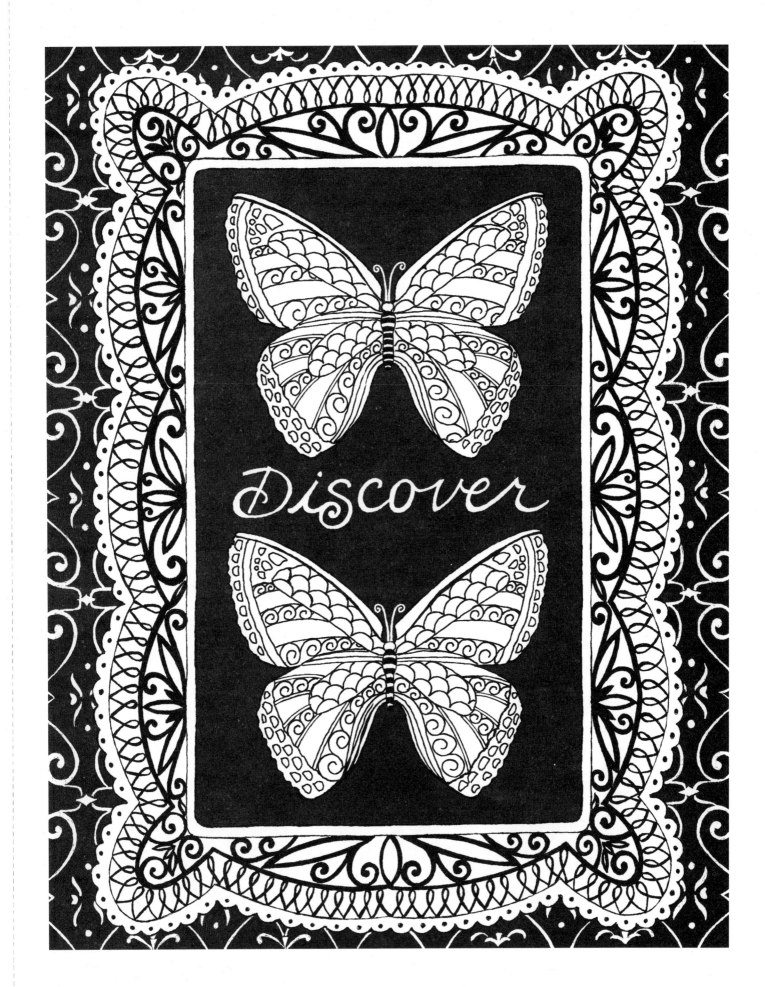

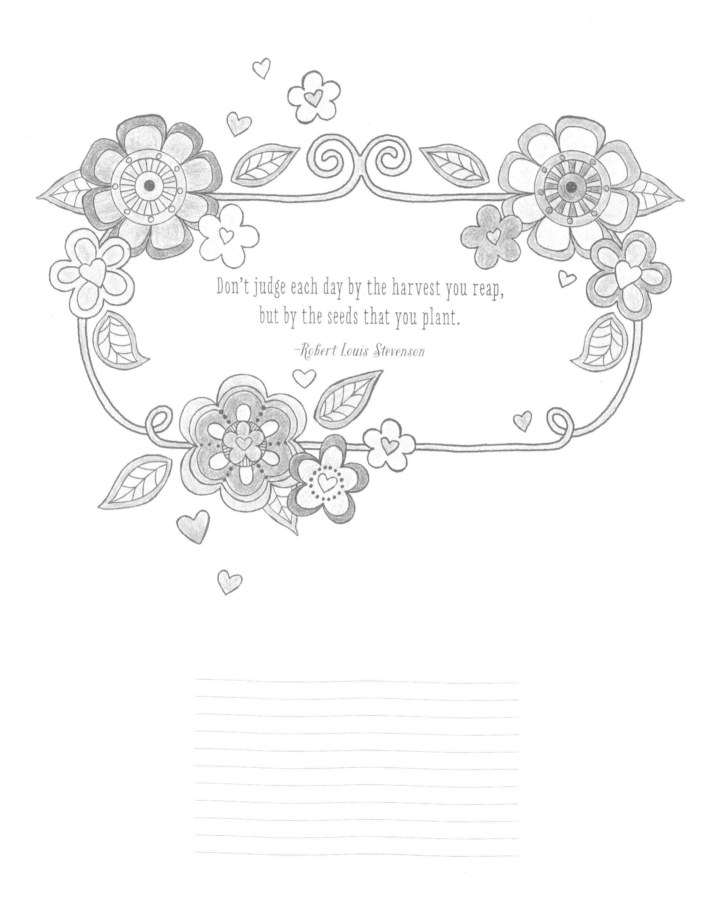

Don't judge each day by the harvest you reap,
but by the seeds that you plant.

–Robert Louis Stevenson

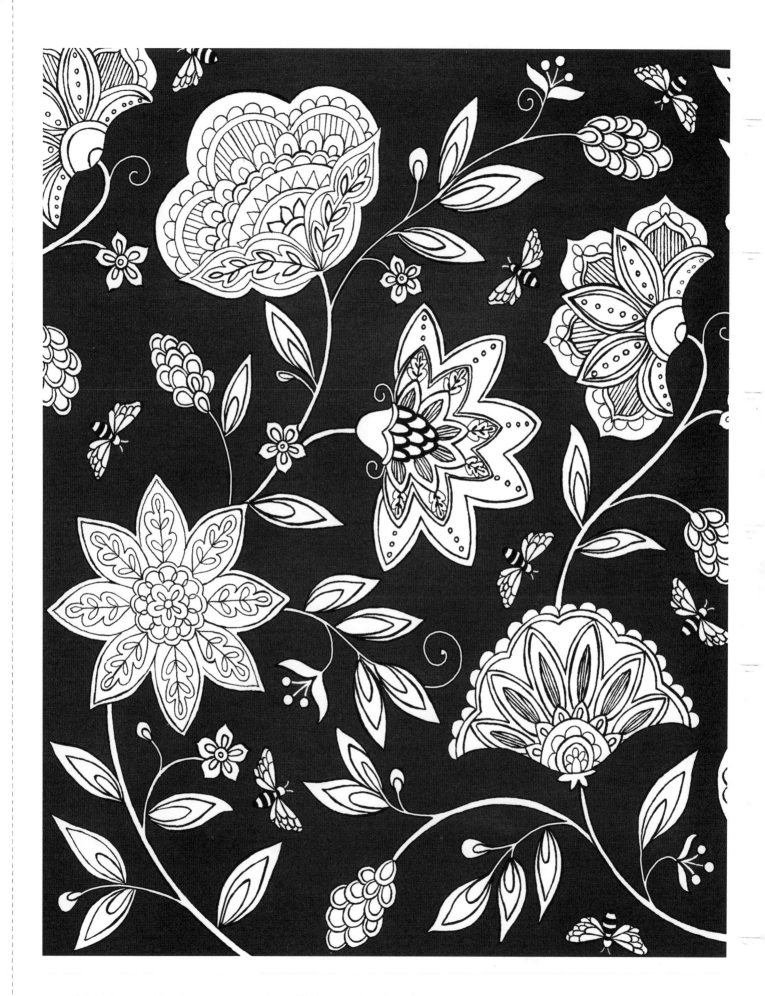

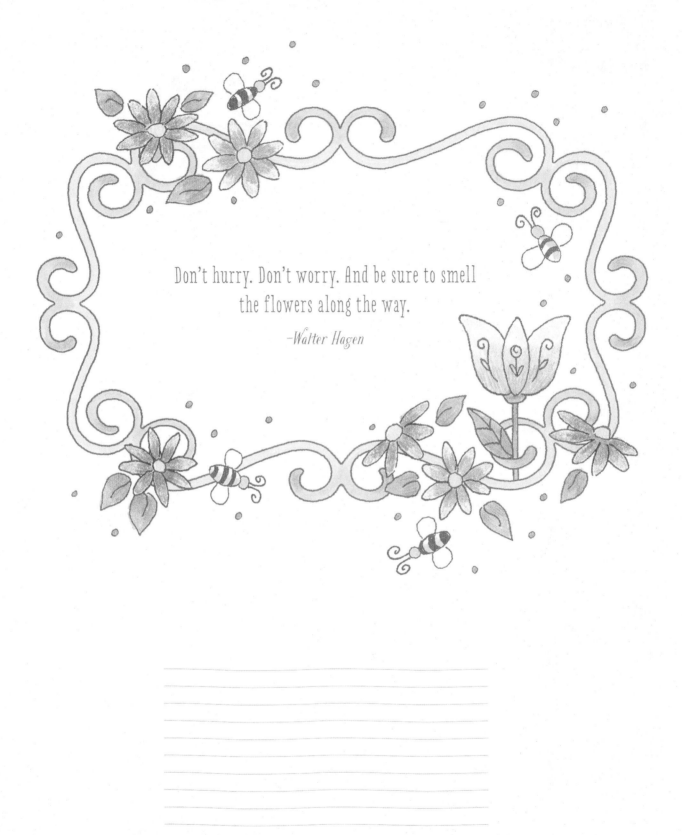

Don't hurry. Don't worry. And be sure to smell the flowers along the way.

–Walter Hagen

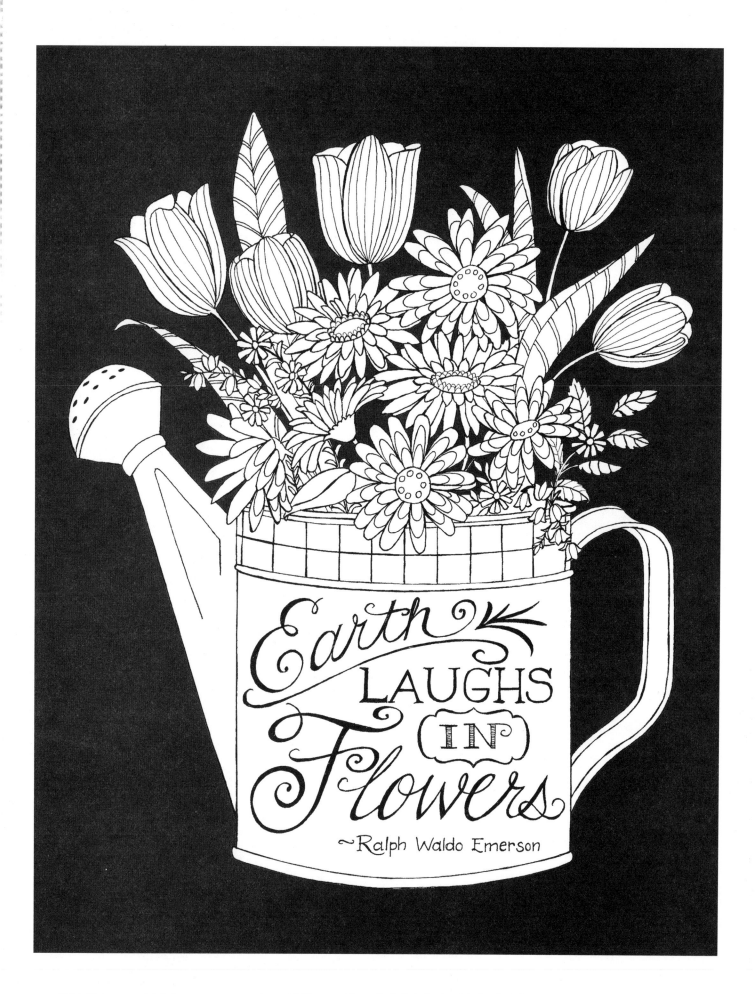

Earth LAUGHS IN Flowers

~Ralph Waldo Emerson

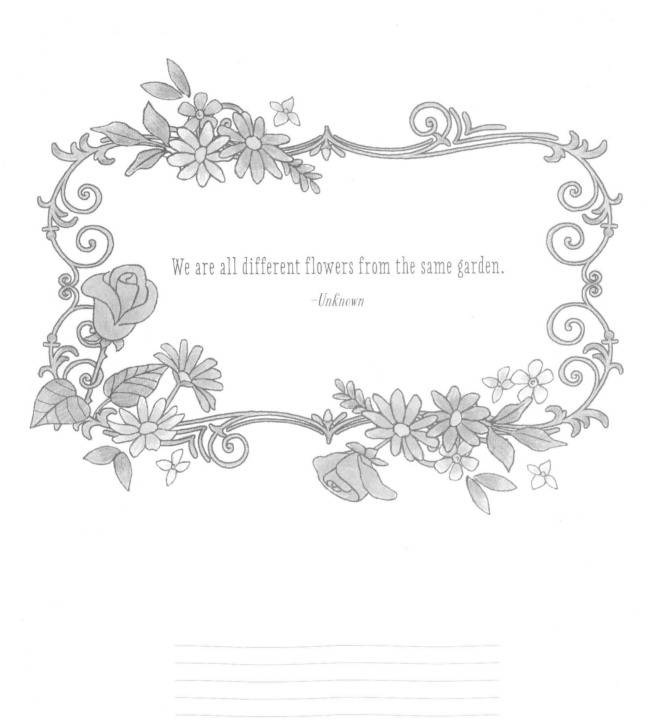

We are all different flowers from the same garden.

–Unknown

_____

_____

_____

_____

_____

_____

_____

_____

_____

_____

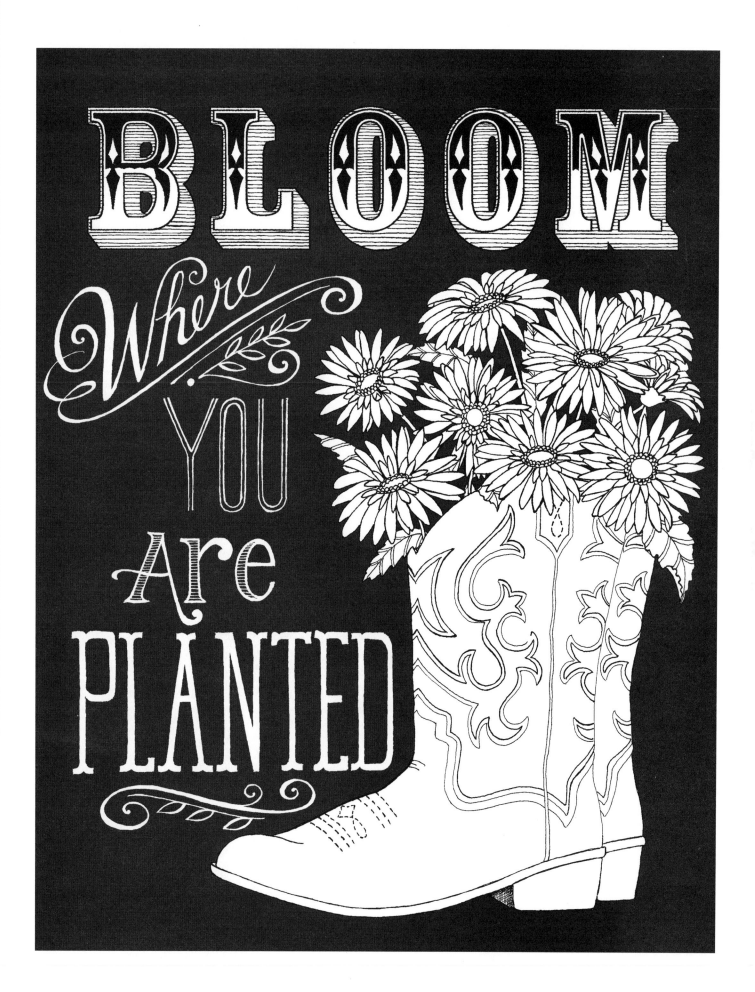

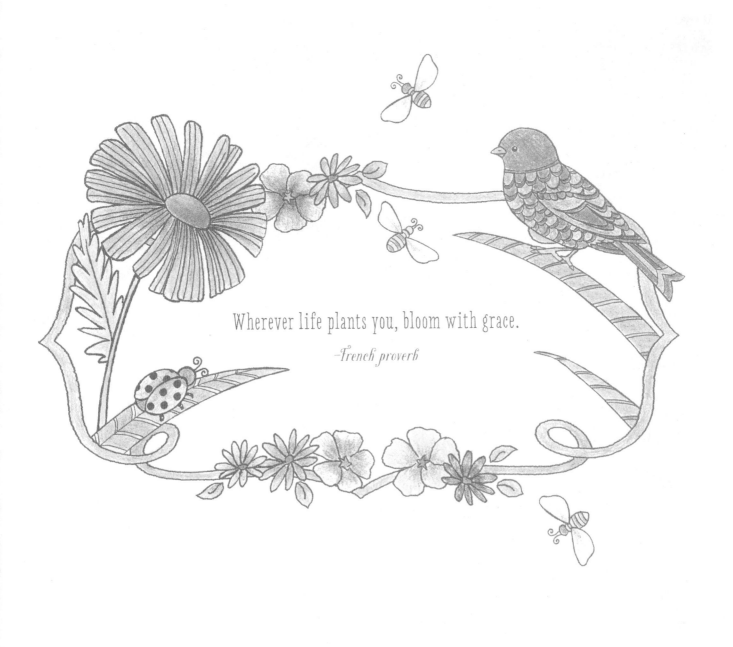

Wherever life plants you, bloom with grace.

—*French proverb*

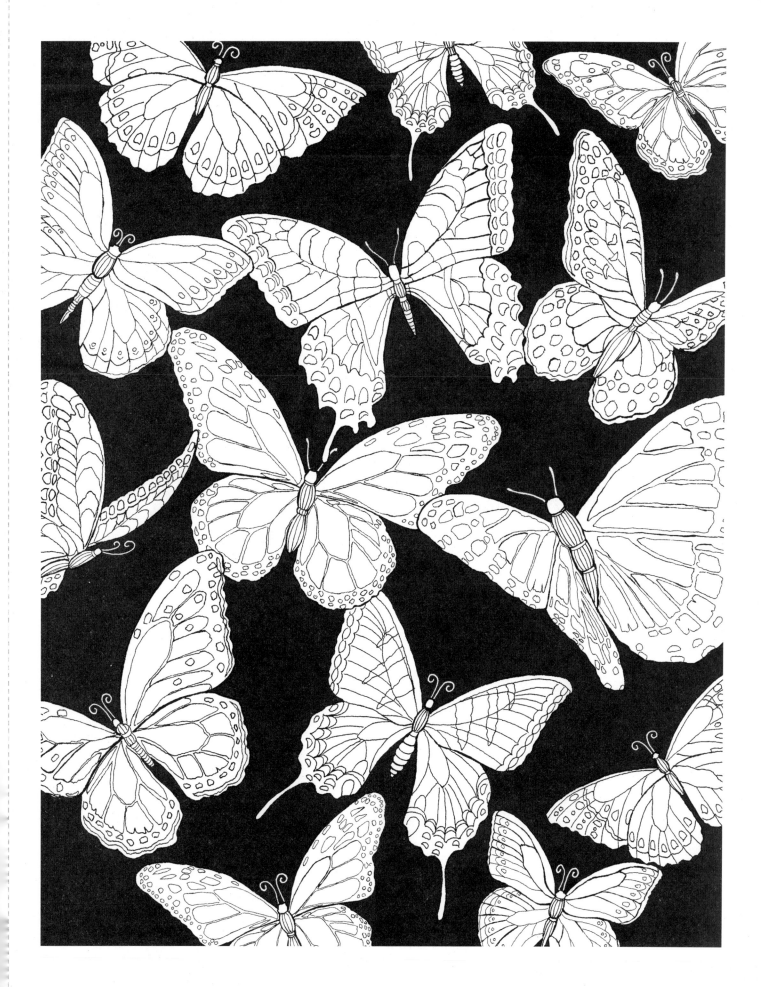

Leave room in your garden for the fairies to dance.

−Unknown

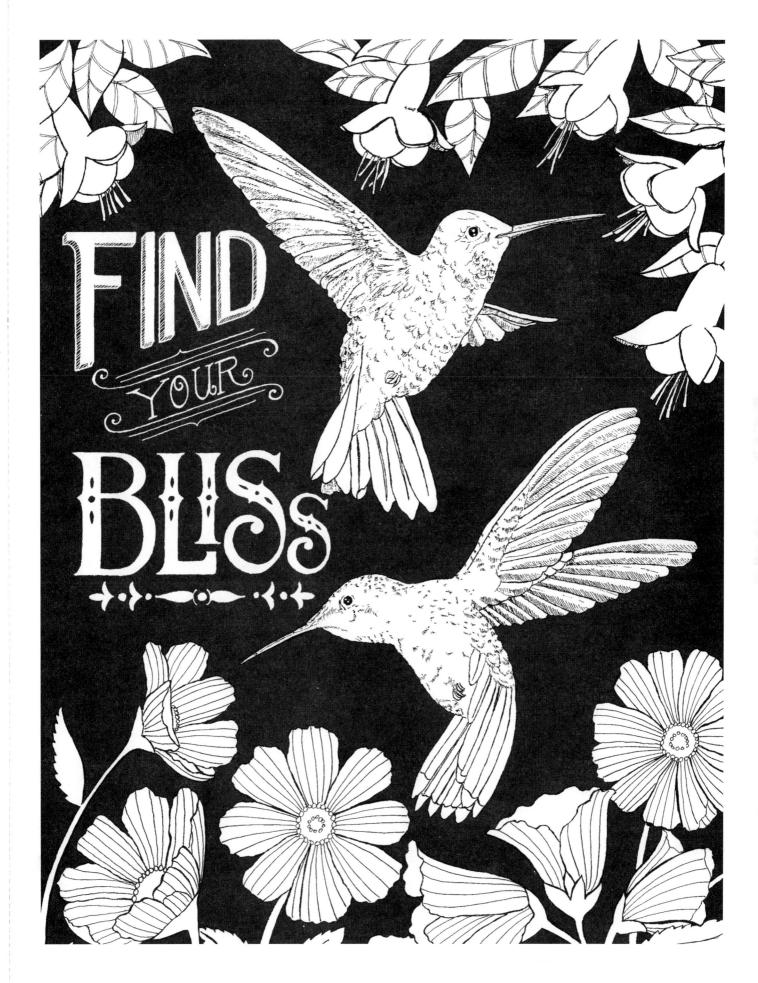

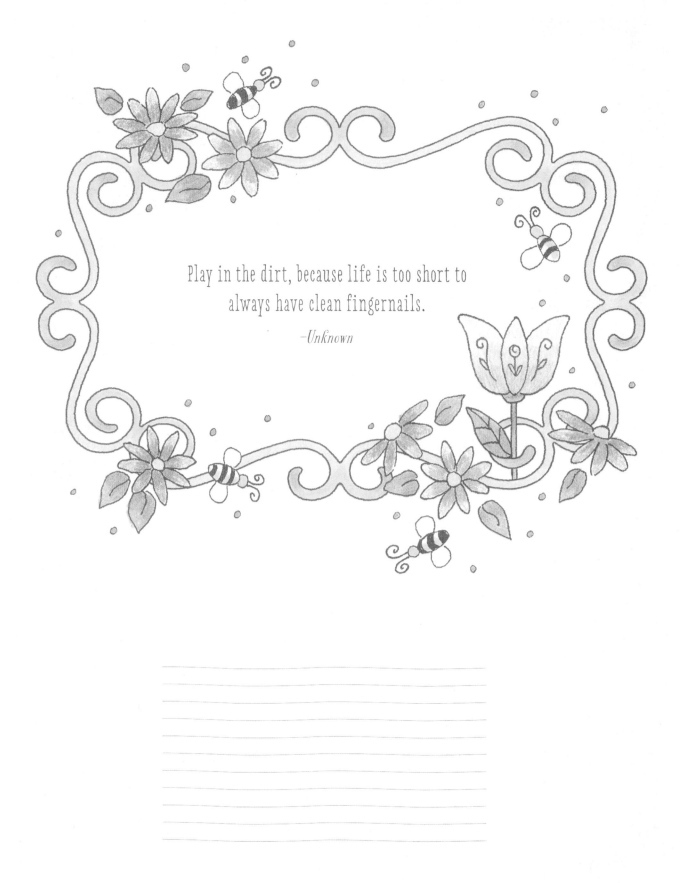

Play in the dirt, because life is too short to
always have clean fingernails.

–Unknown

_____

_____

_____

_____

_____

_____

_____

_____

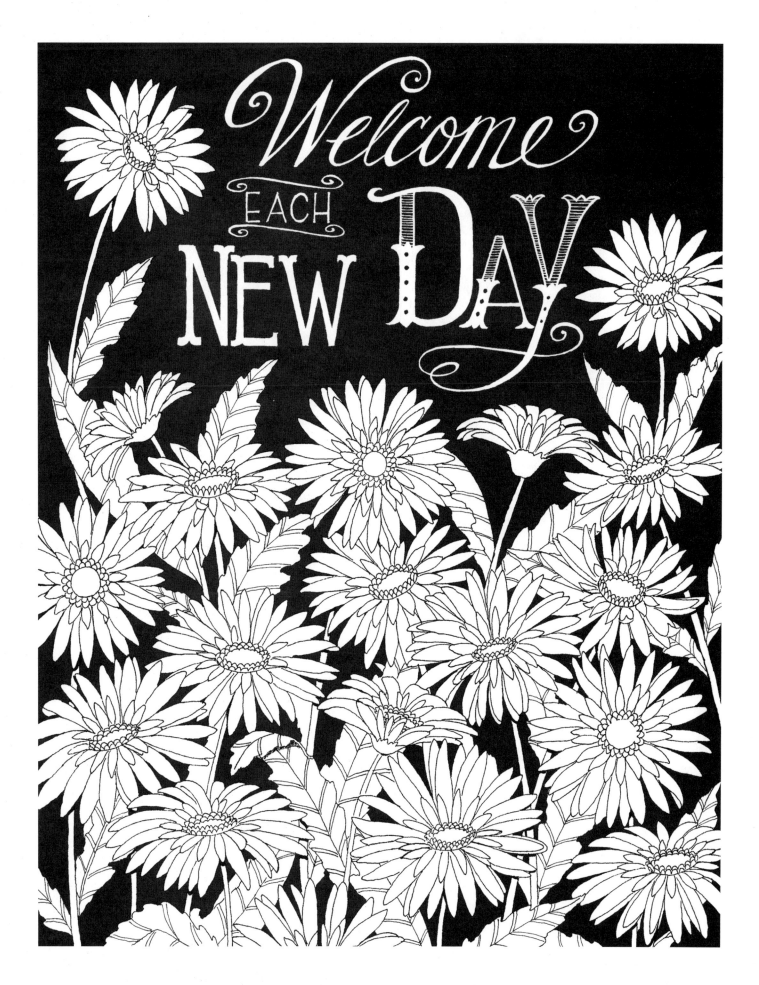

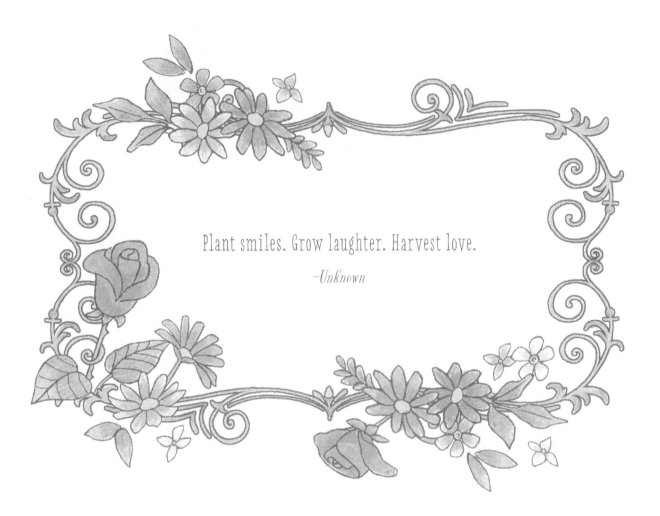

Plant smiles. Grow laughter. Harvest love.

–Unknown

_____

_____

_____

_____

_____

_____

_____

_____

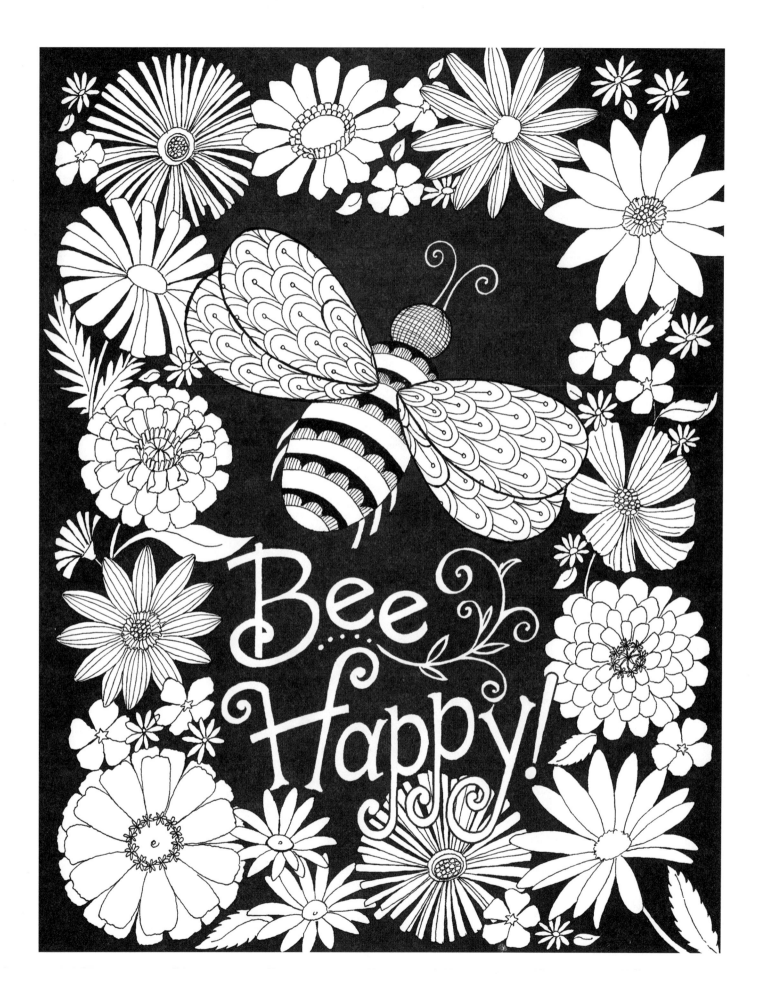

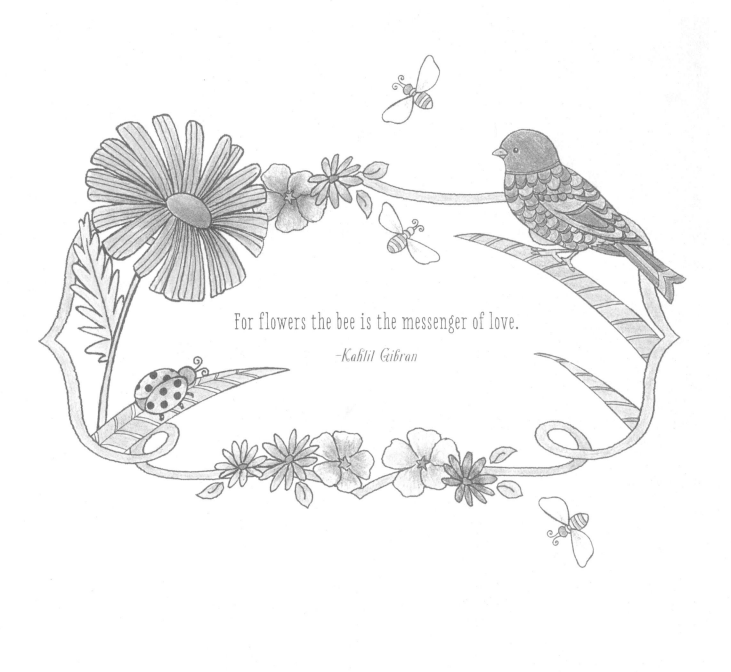

For flowers the bee is the messenger of love.

–Kahlil Gibran

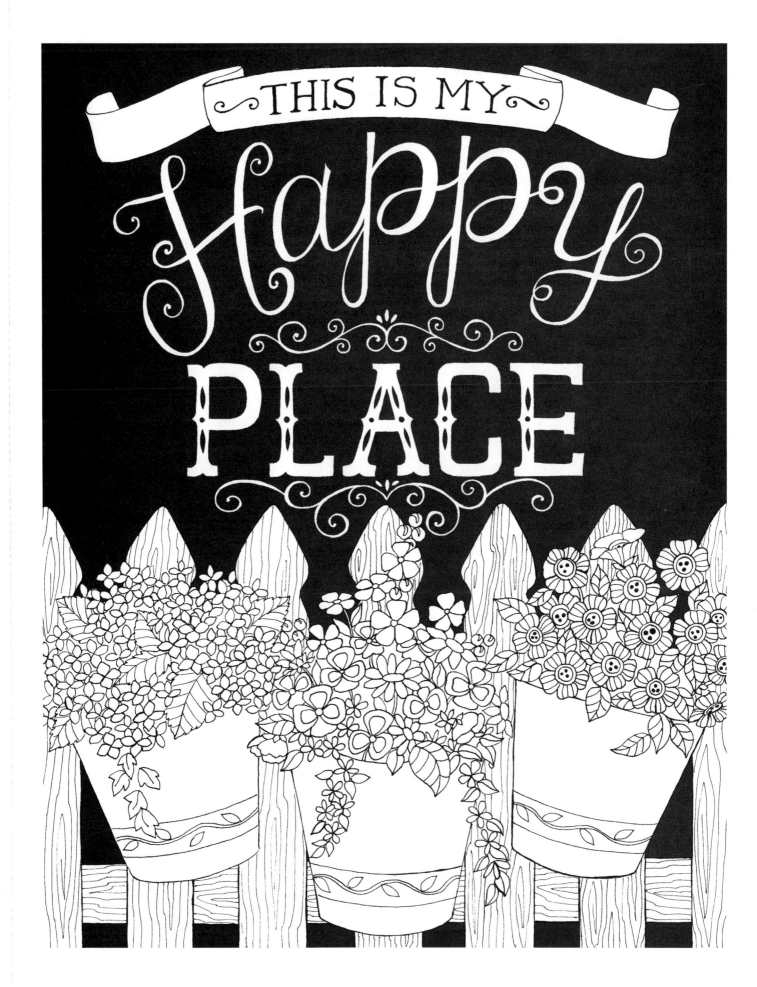

My garden of flowers is also my garden of thoughts and dreams.

–Unknown

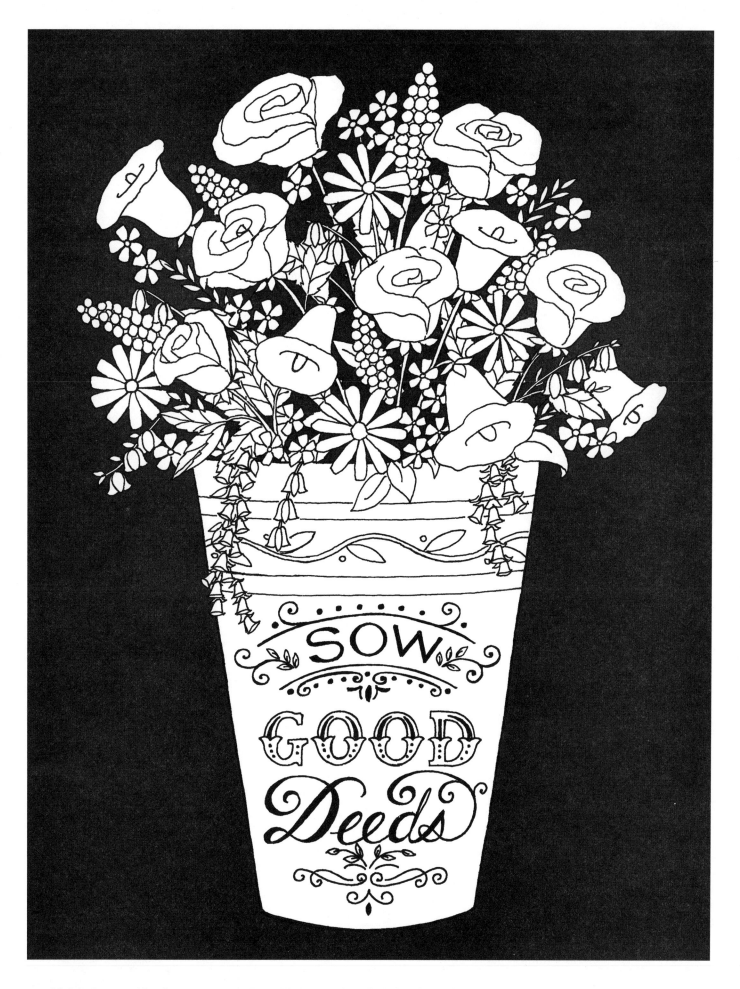

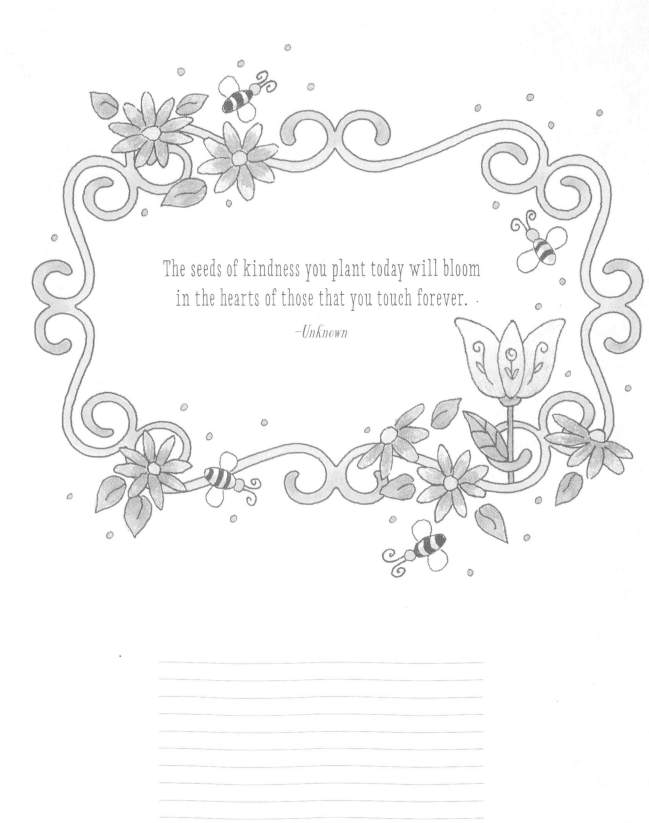

The seeds of kindness you plant today will bloom
in the hearts of those that you touch forever.

—Unknown

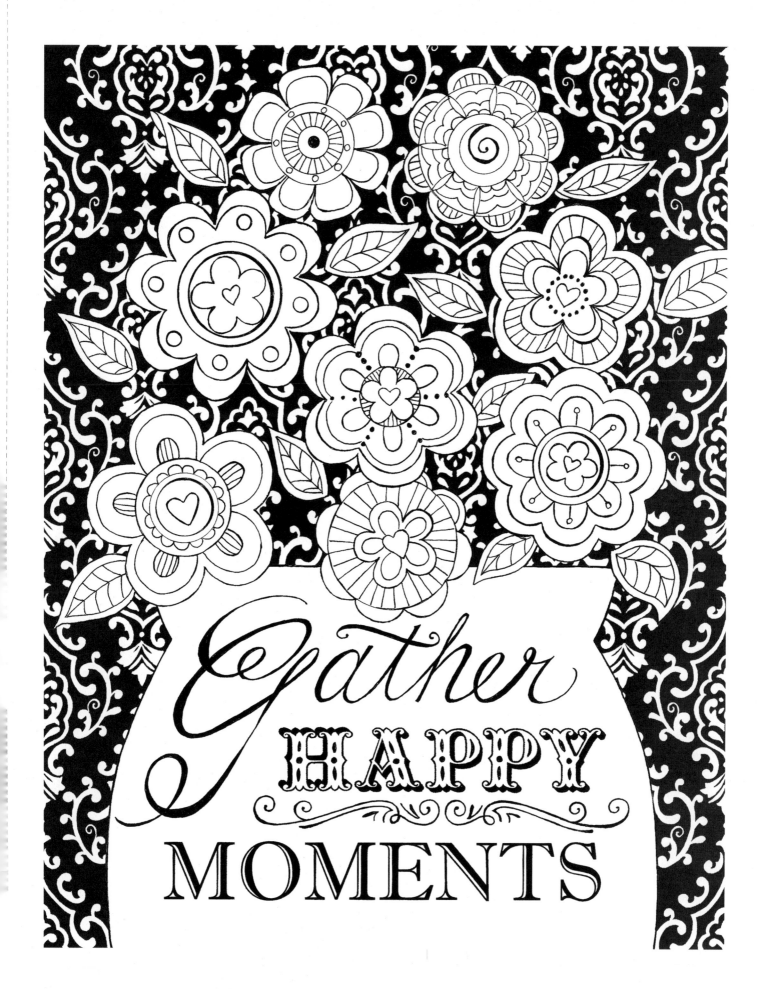

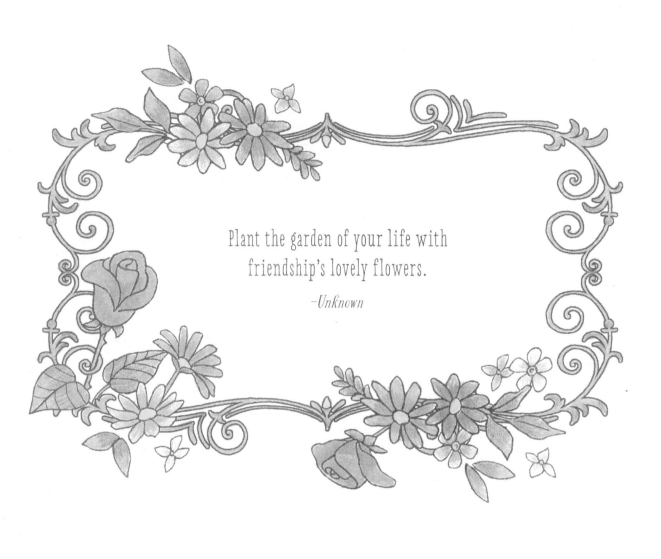

Plant the garden of your life with
friendship's lovely flowers.

–Unknown

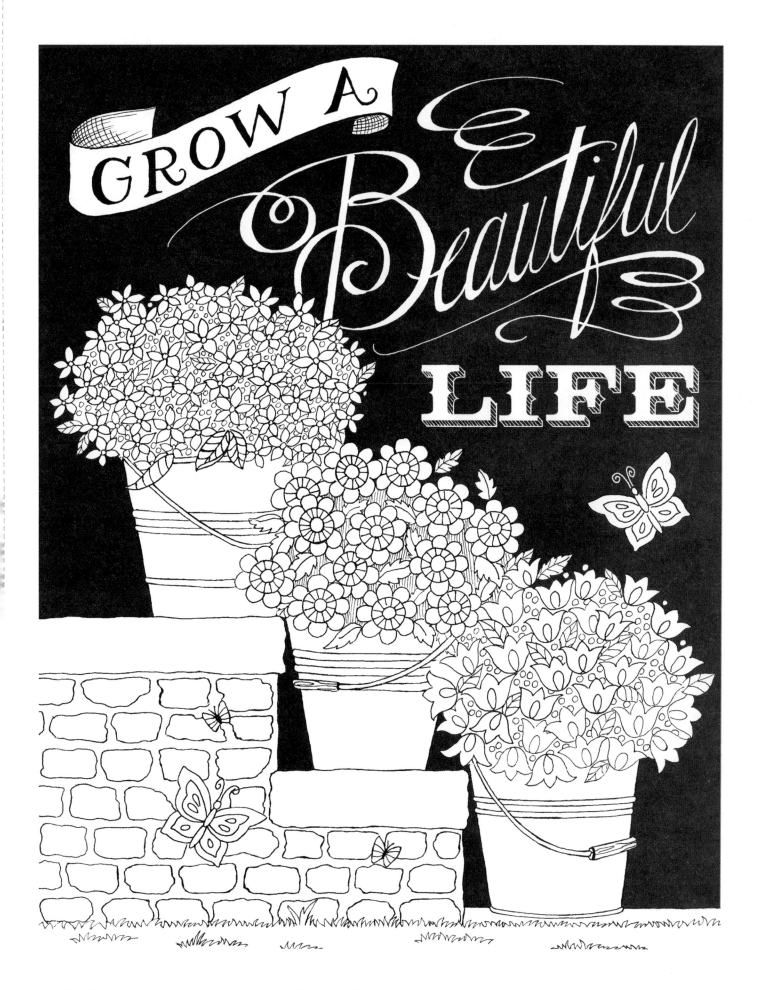

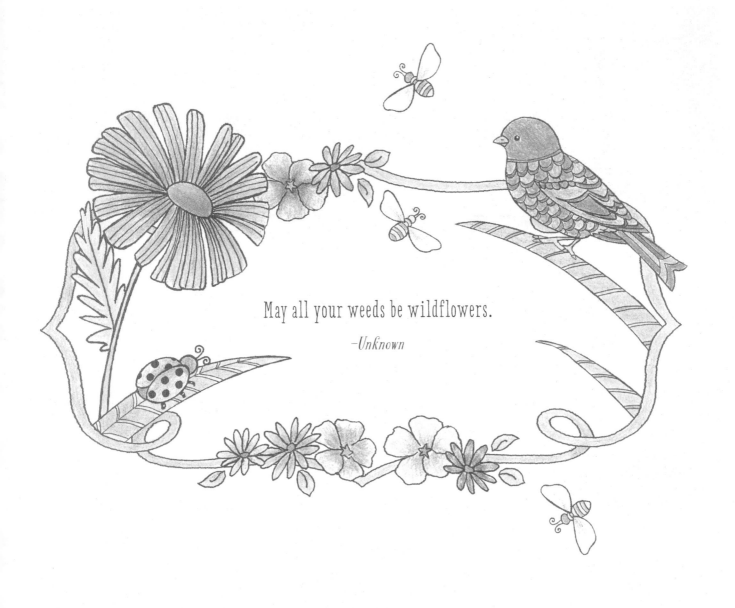

May all your weeds be wildflowers.

—Unknown

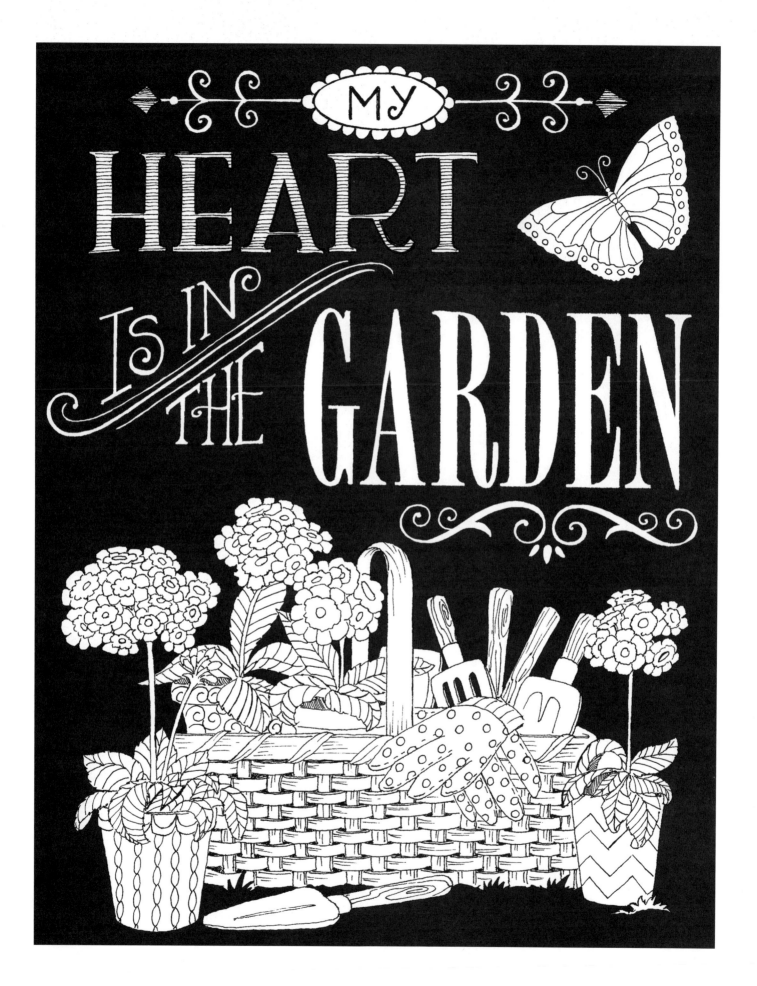

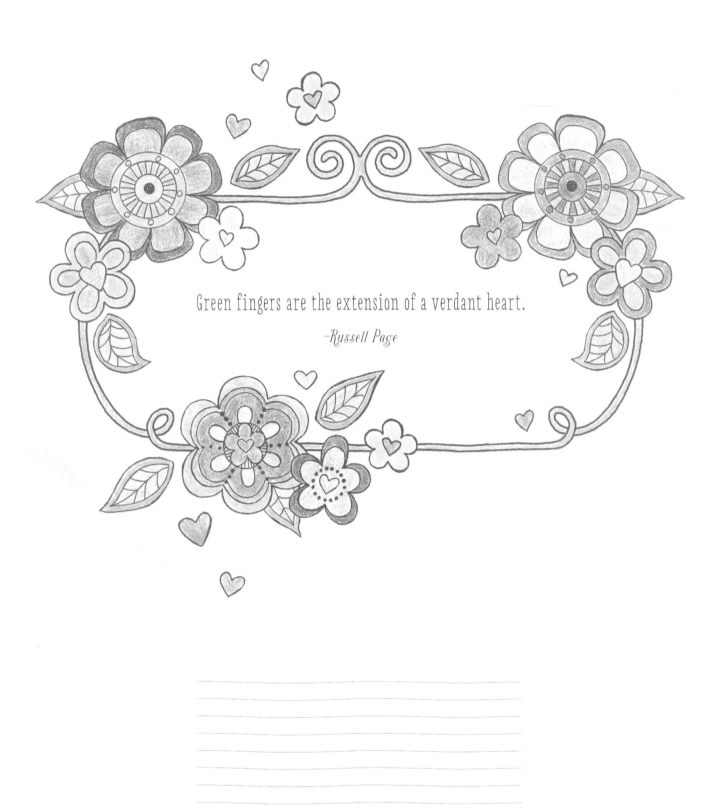

Green fingers are the extension of a verdant heart.

—Russell Page

_____

_____

_____

_____

_____

_____

_____

_____

_____

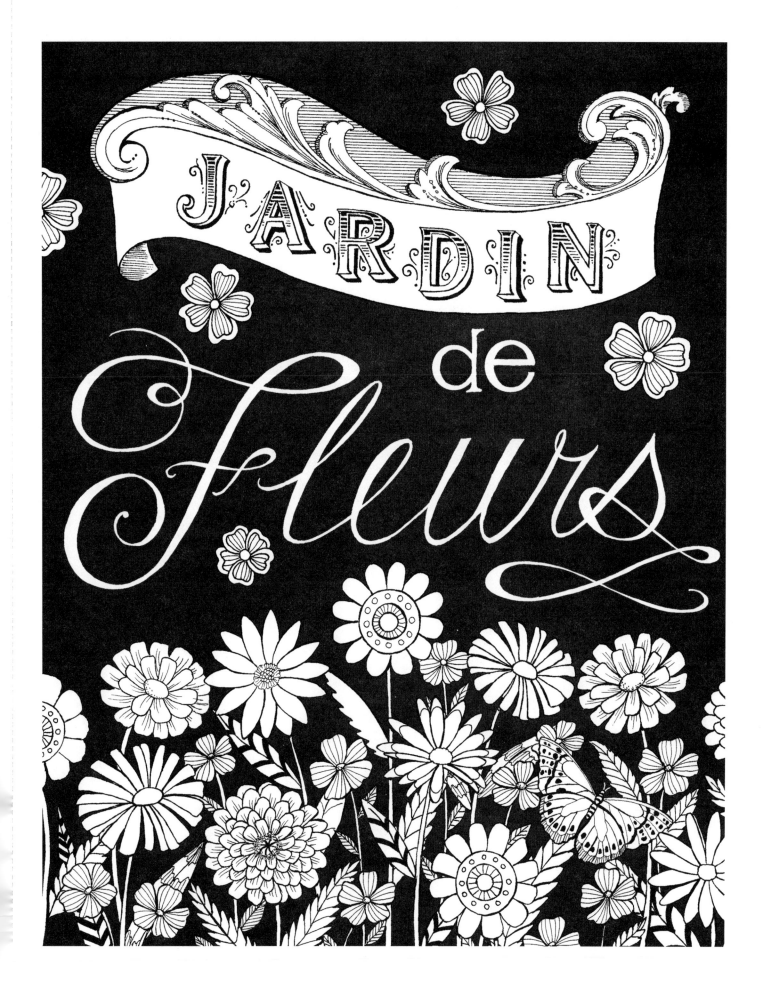

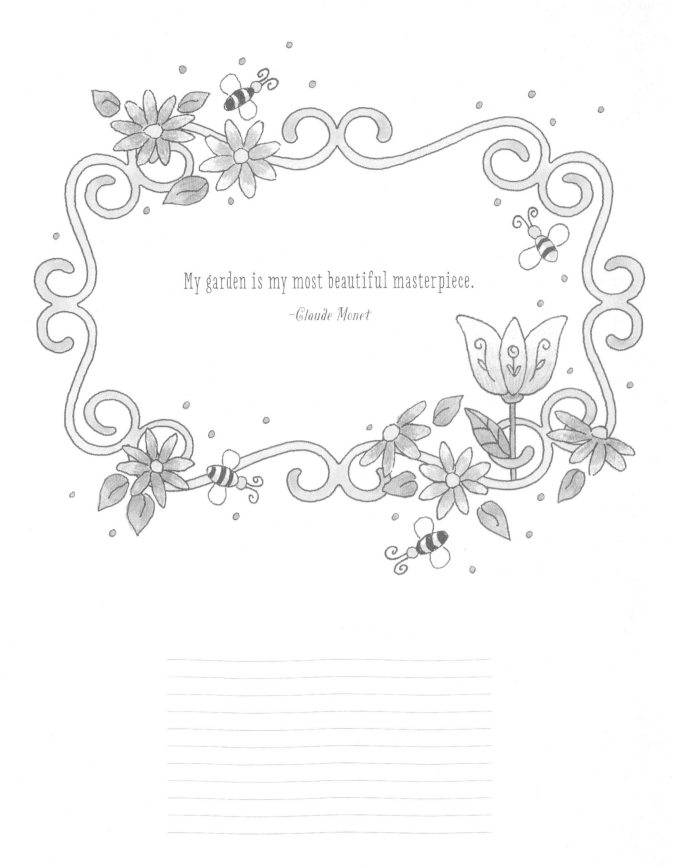

My garden is my most beautiful masterpiece.

–Claude Monet

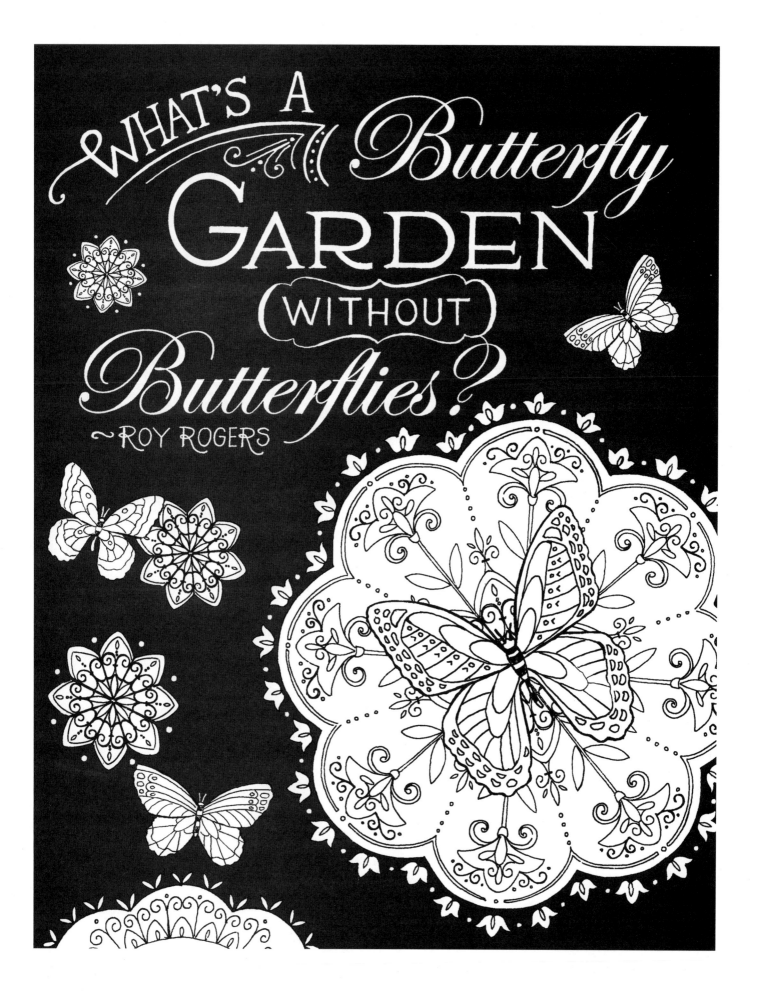

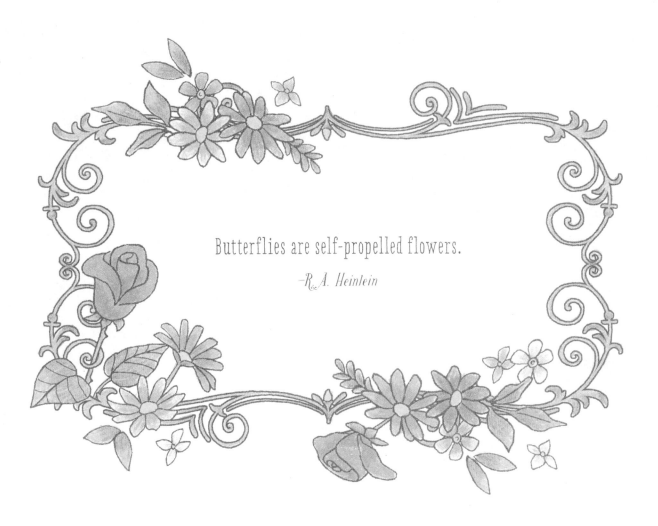

Butterflies are self-propelled flowers.

-R. A. Heinlein

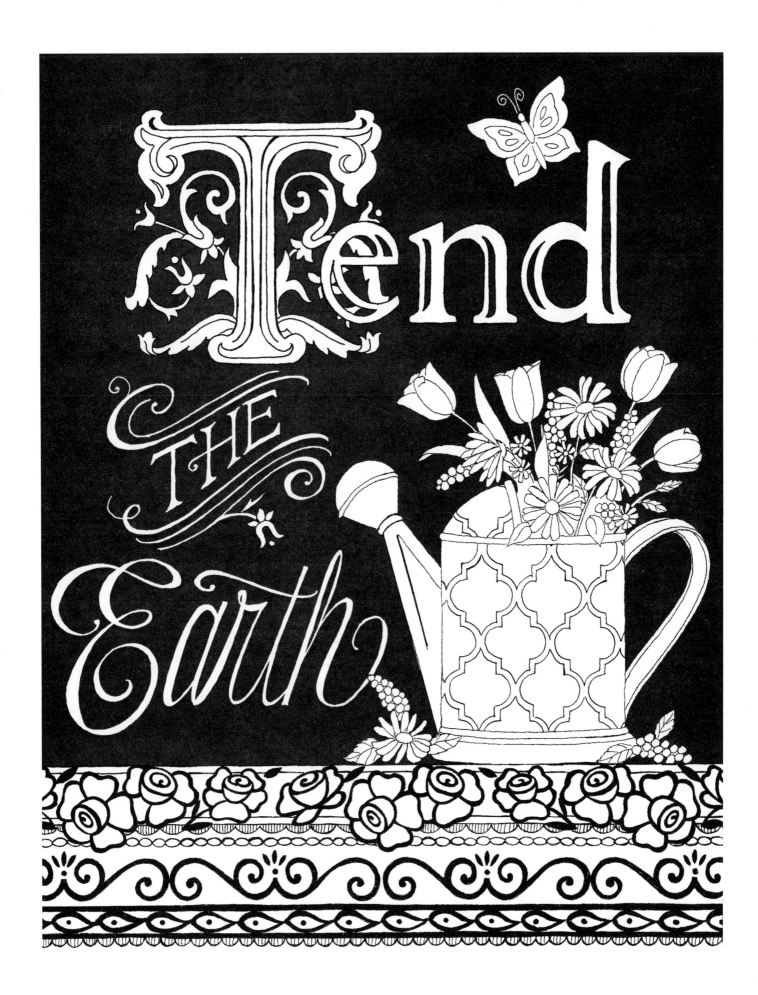

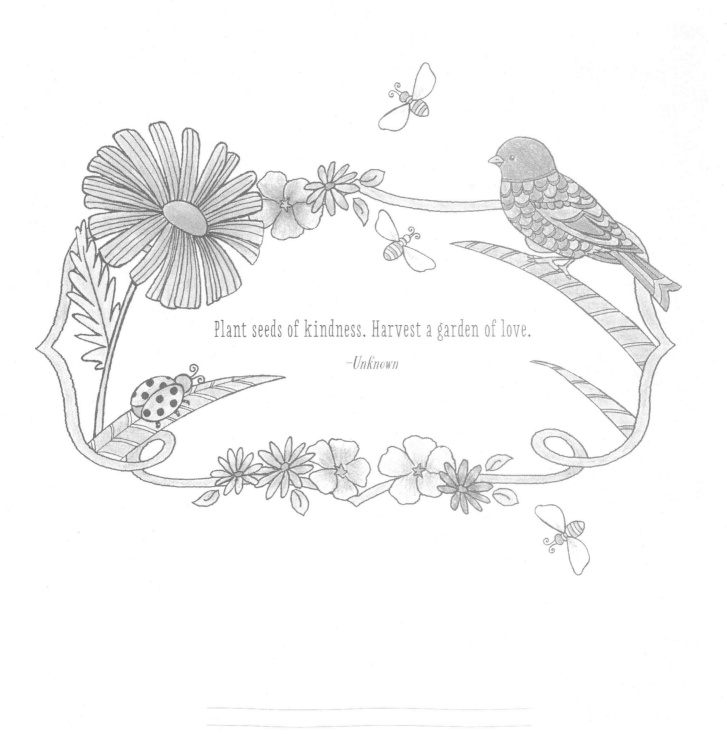

Plant seeds of kindness. Harvest a garden of love.

–Unknown

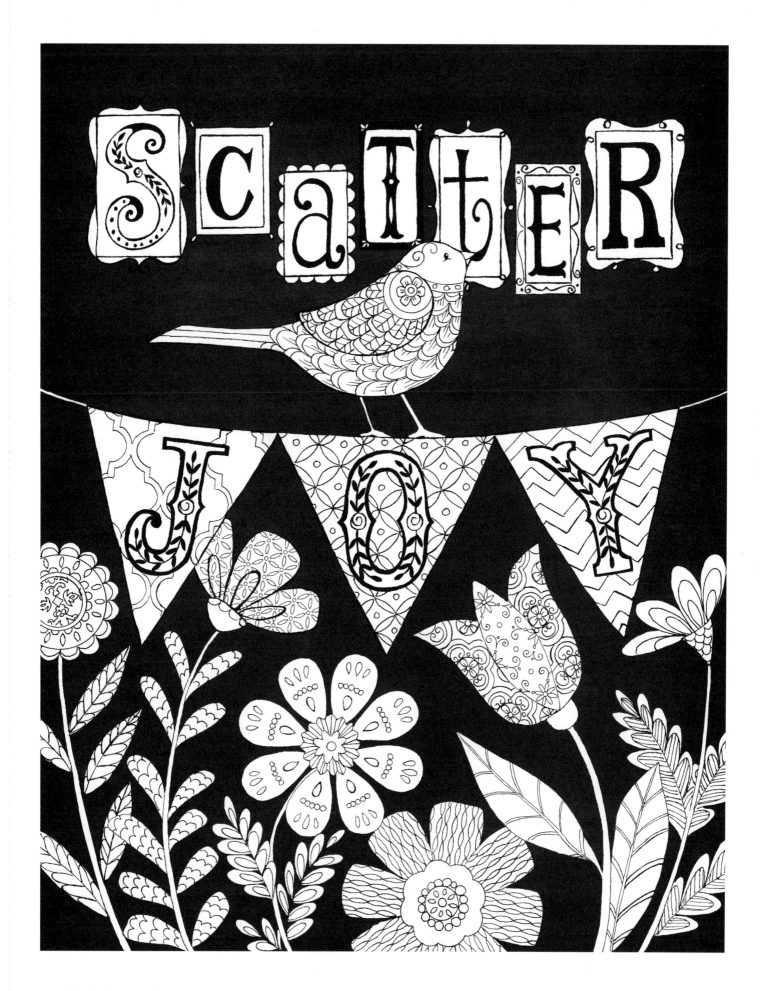

Joy is not in things; it is in us.

—Richard Wagner

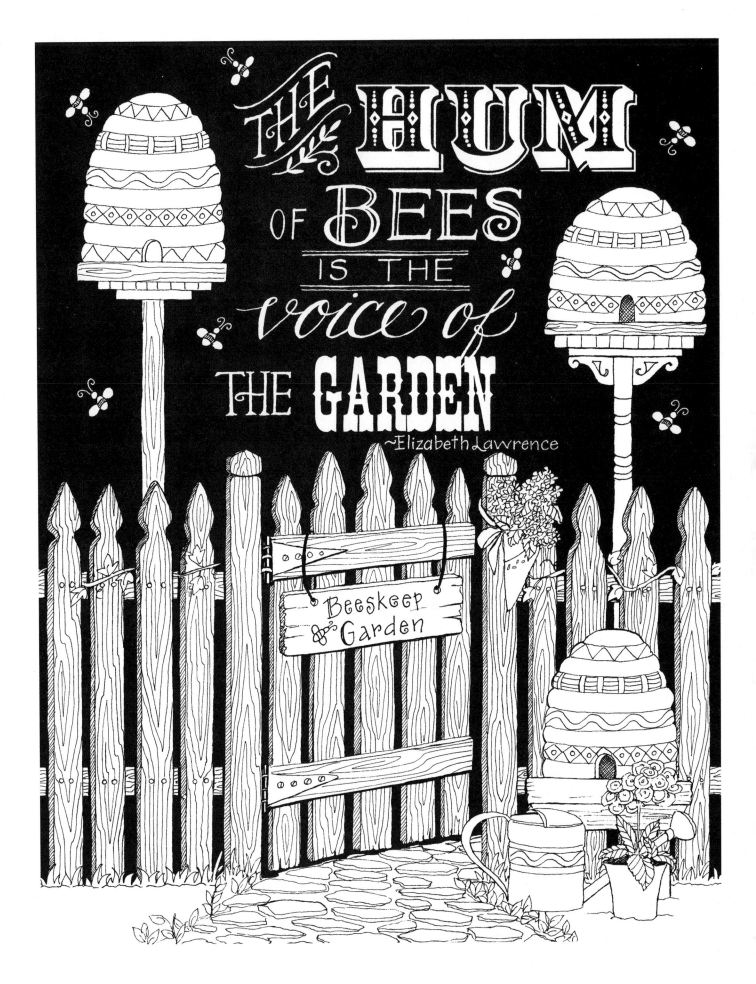

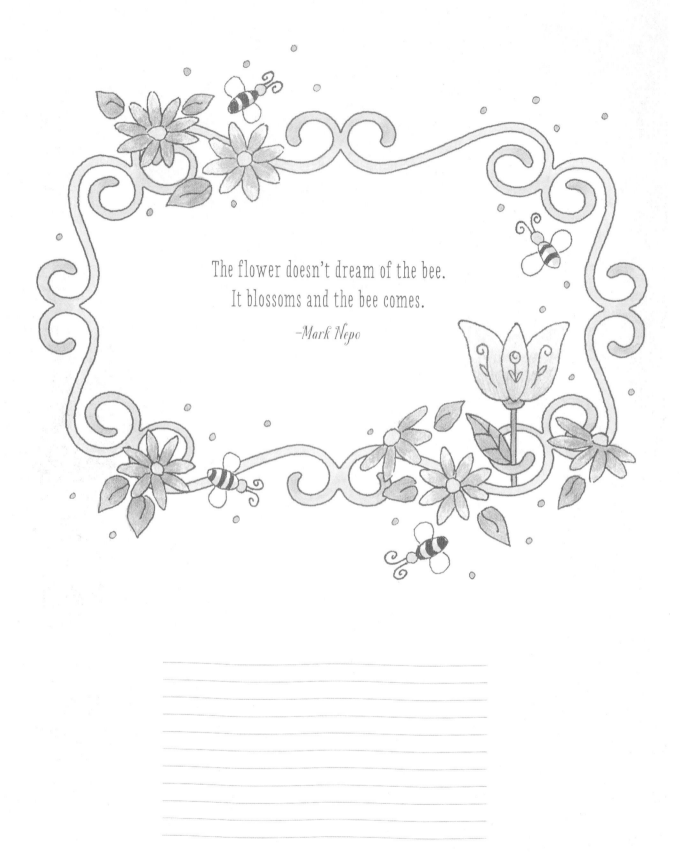

The flower doesn't dream of the bee.
It blossoms and the bee comes.

–Mark Nepo

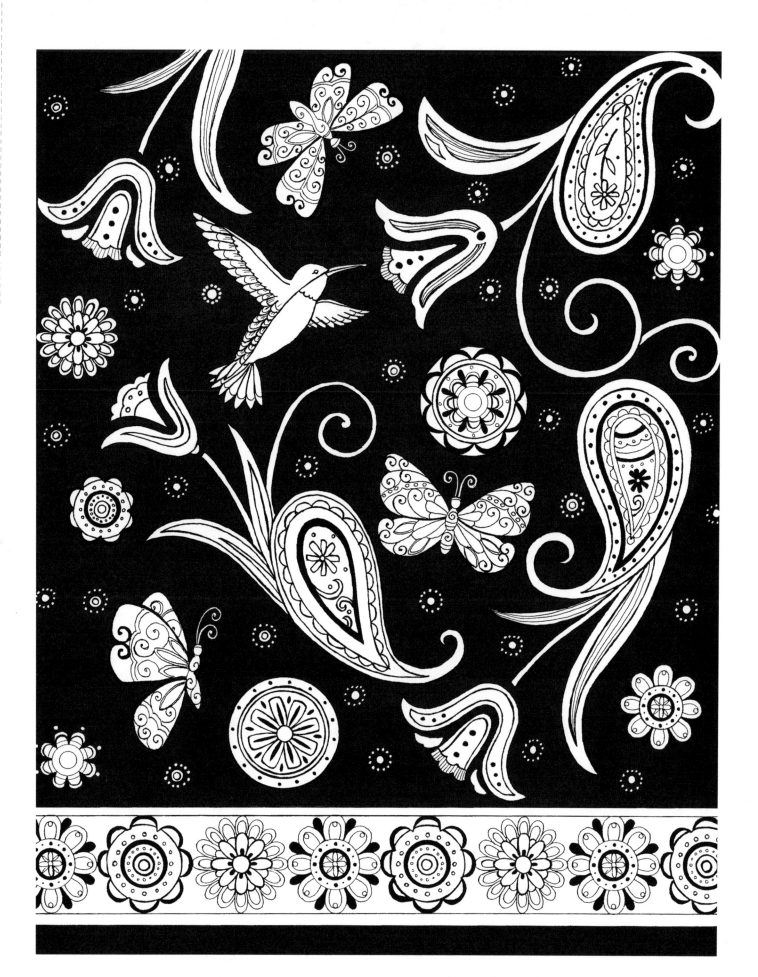

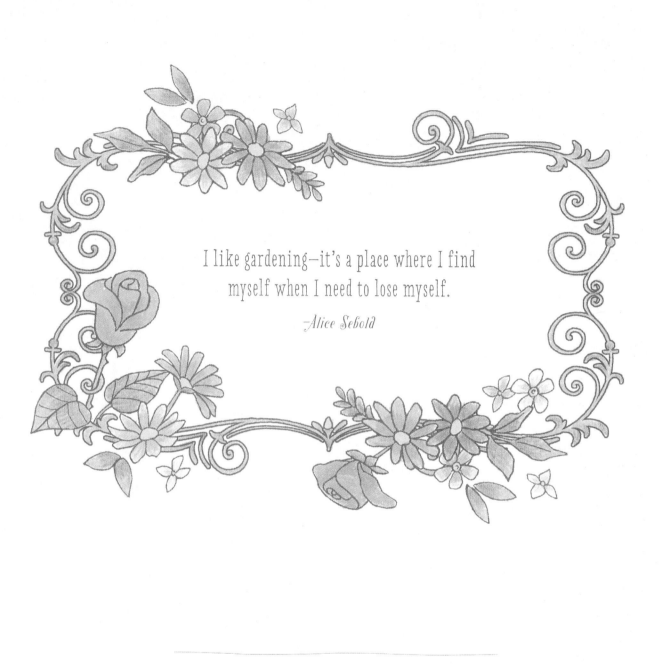

I like gardening—it's a place where I find
myself when I need to lose myself.

—*Alice Sebold*

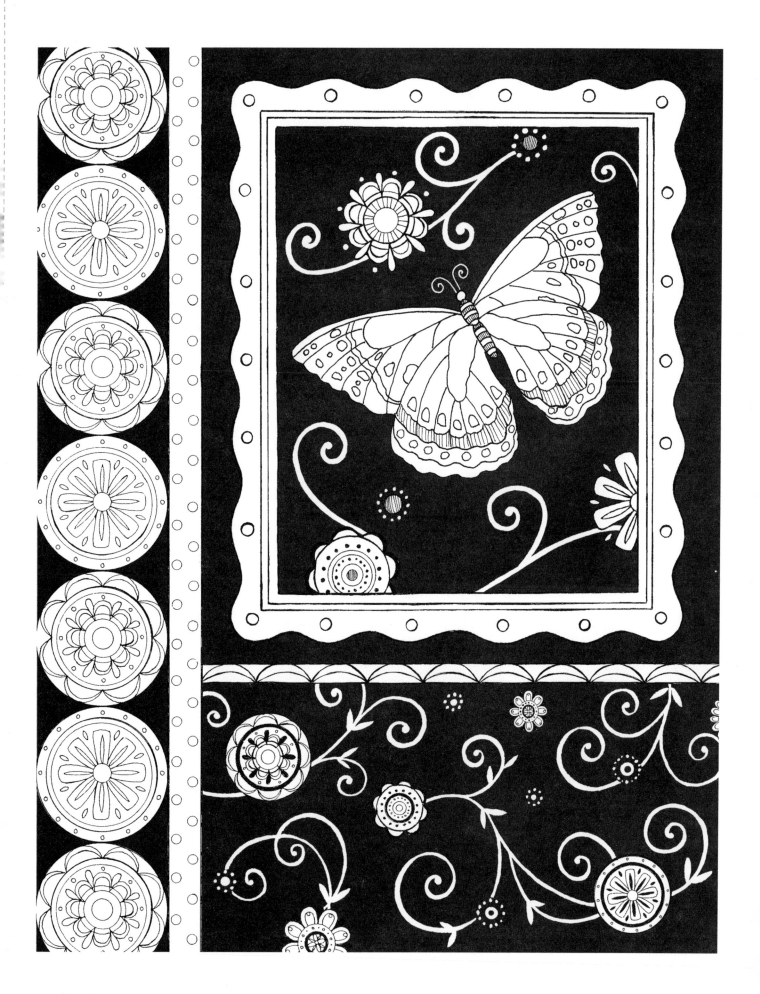

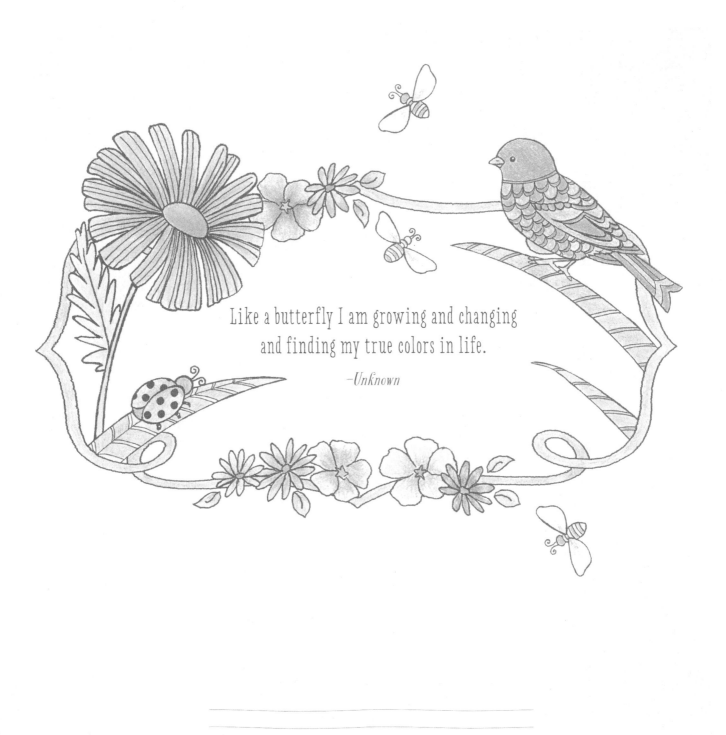

Like a butterfly I am growing and changing
and finding my true colors in life.

—*Unknown*

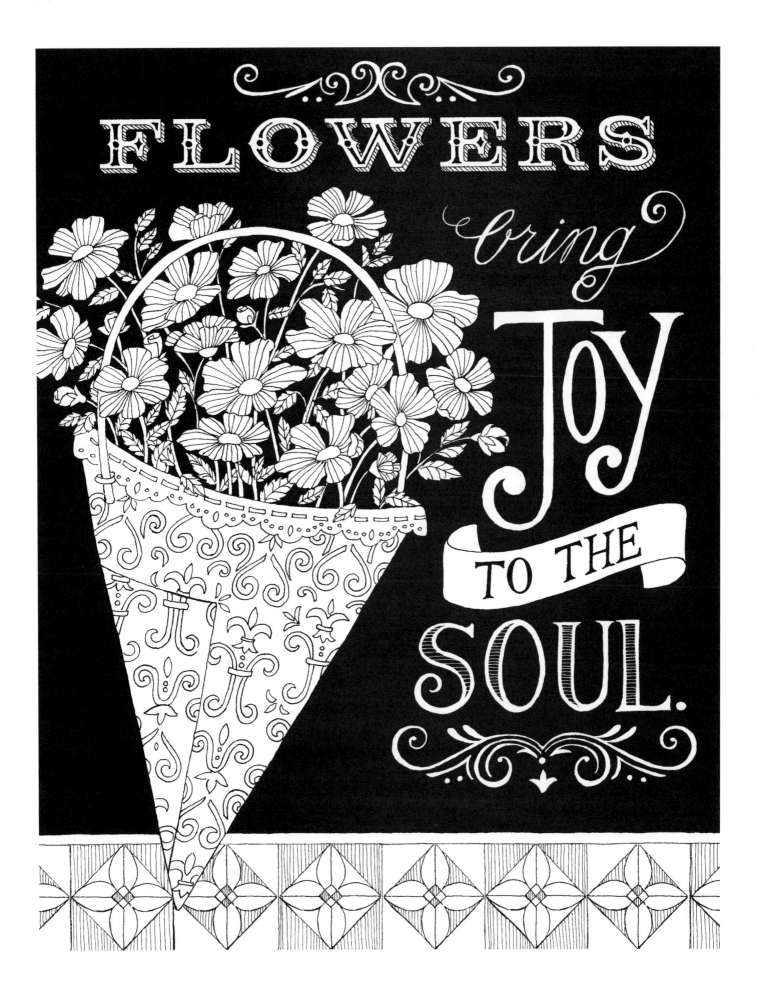

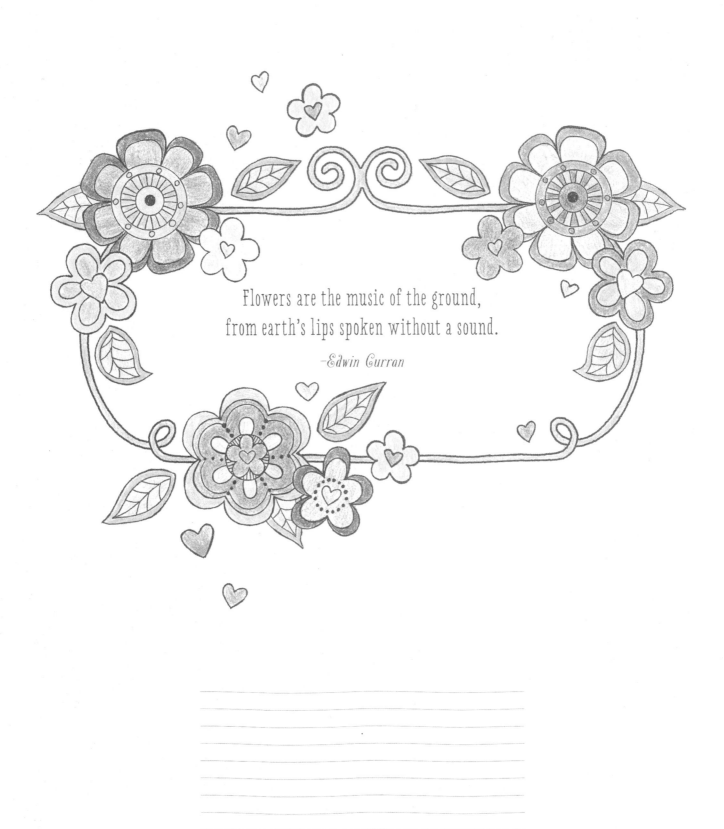

Flowers are the music of the ground,
from earth's lips spoken without a sound.

—Edwin Curran

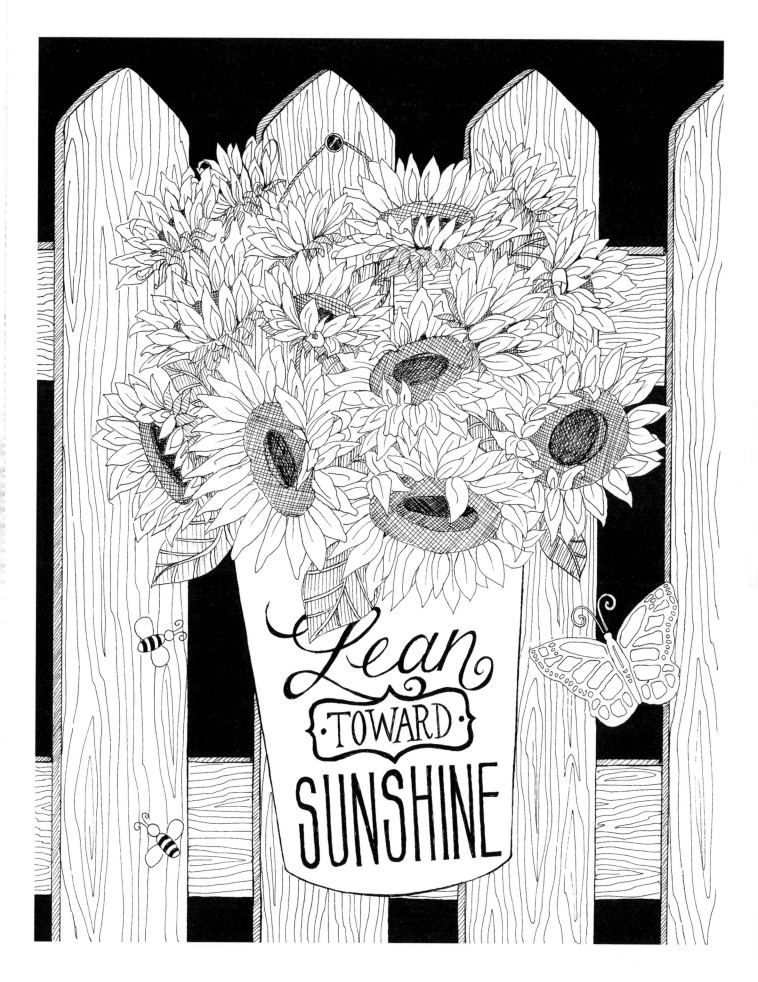

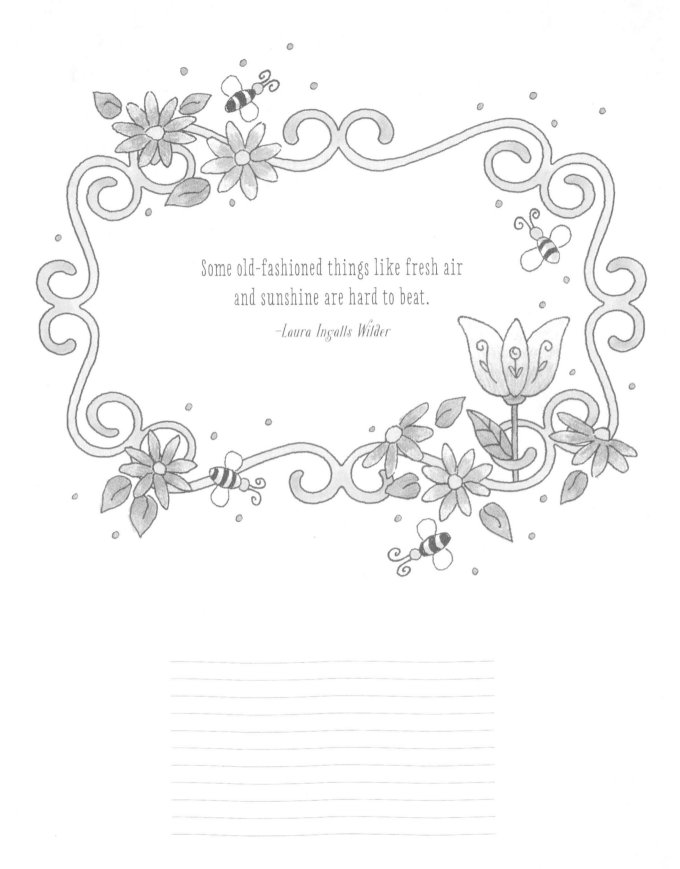

Some old-fashioned things like fresh air
and sunshine are hard to beat.

–Laura Ingalls Wilder

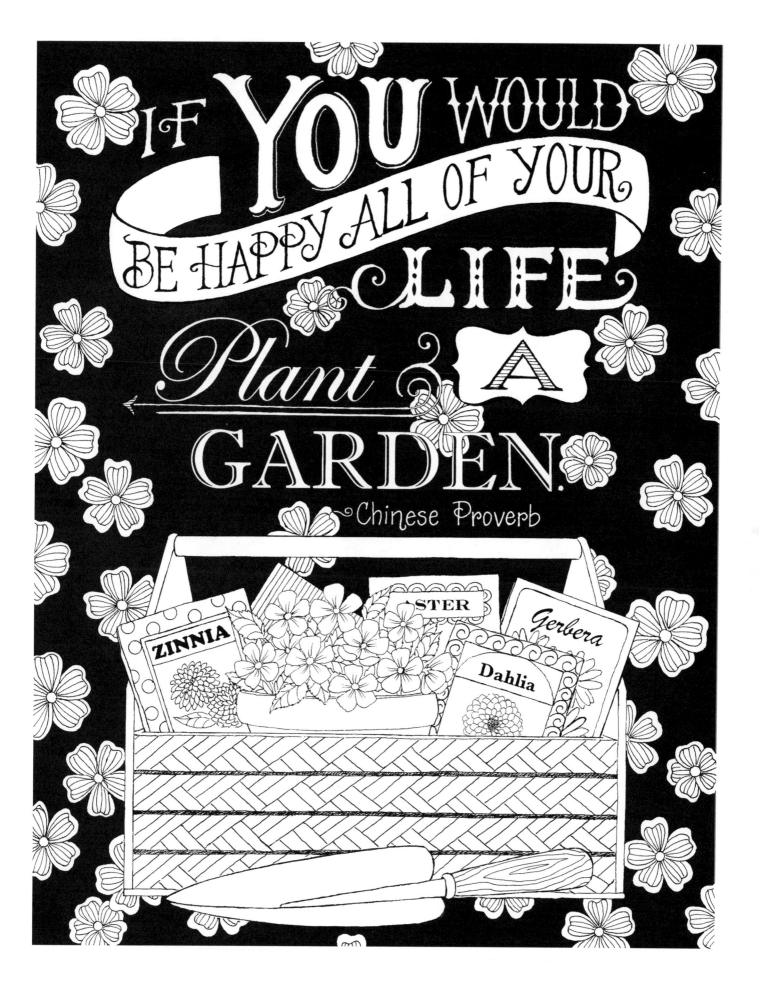

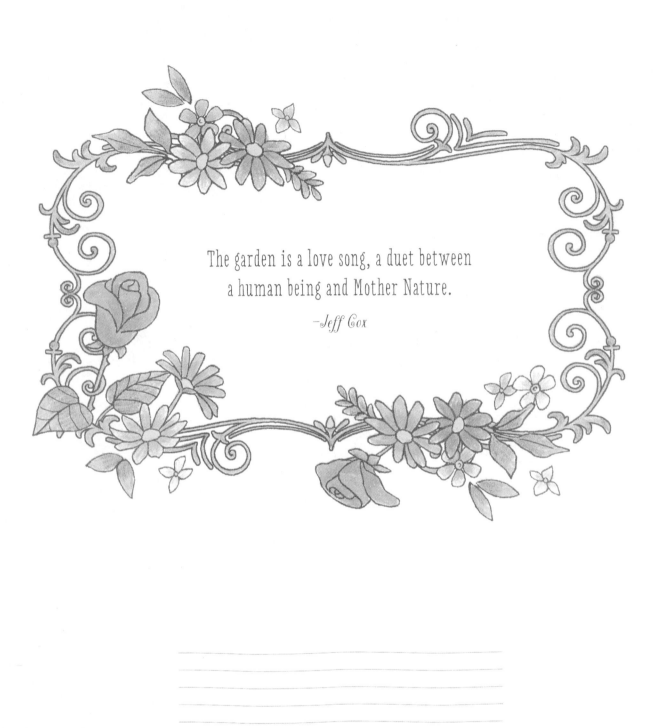

The garden is a love song, a duet between
a human being and Mother Nature.

−Jeff Cox

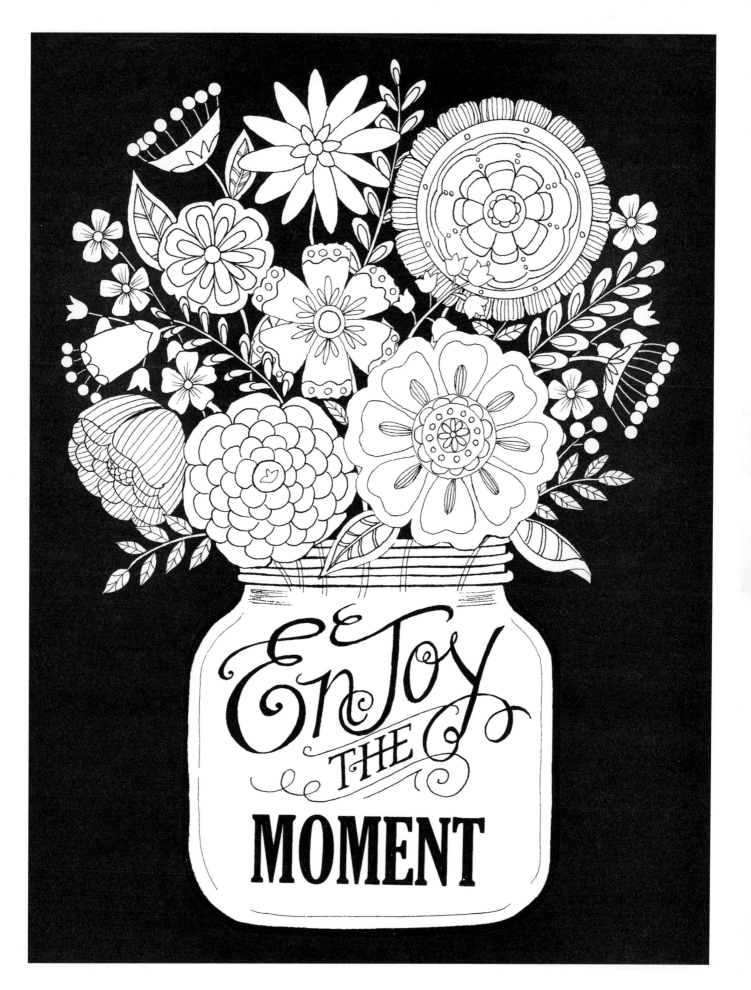

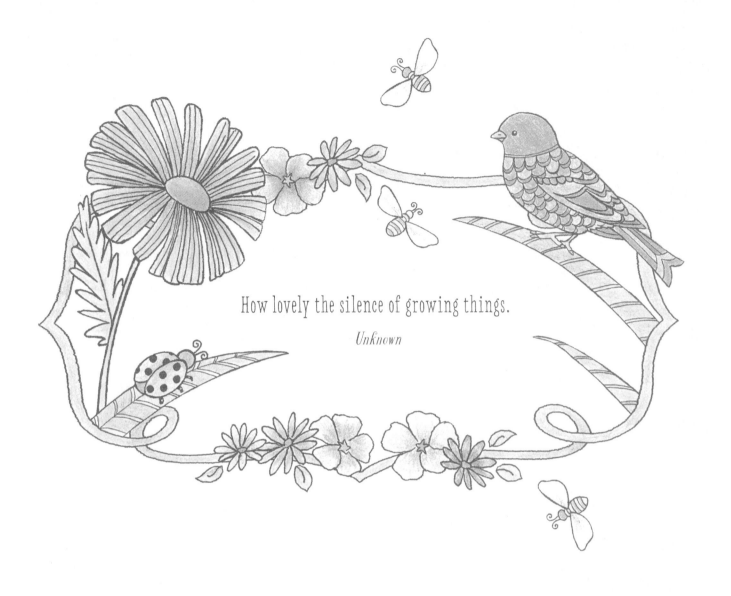

How lovely the silence of growing things.

Unknown

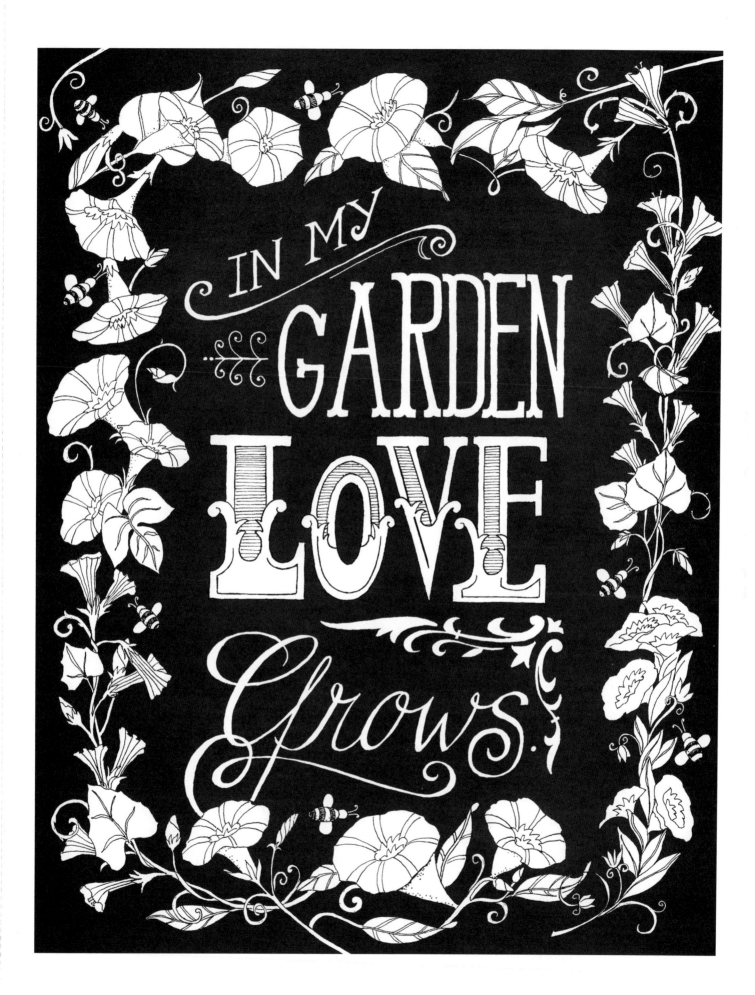

IN MY GARDEN LOVE Grows.

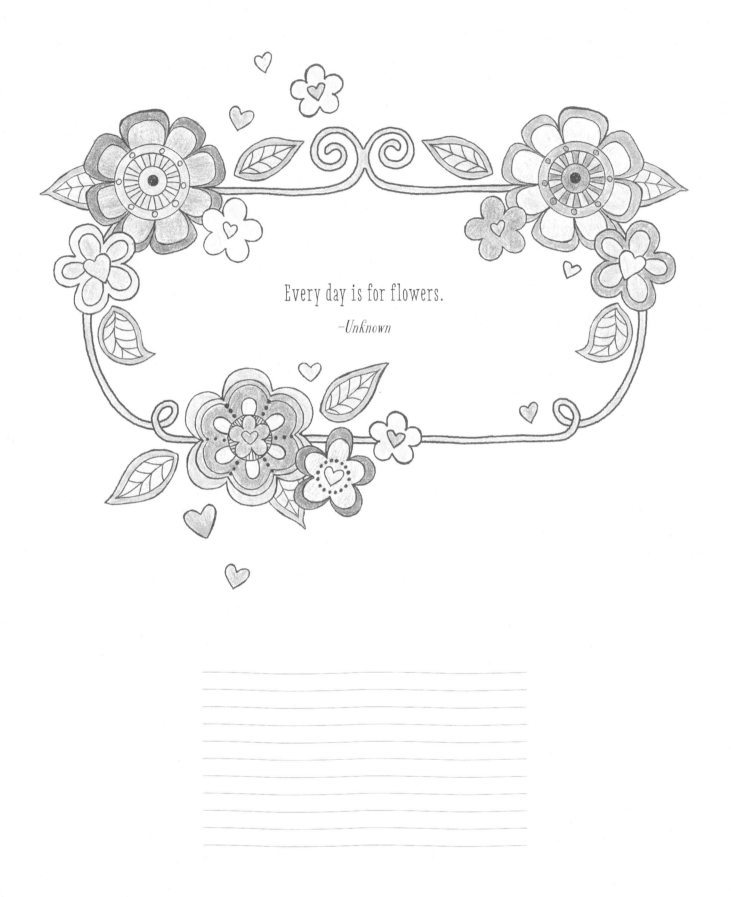

Every day is for flowers.
—Unknown

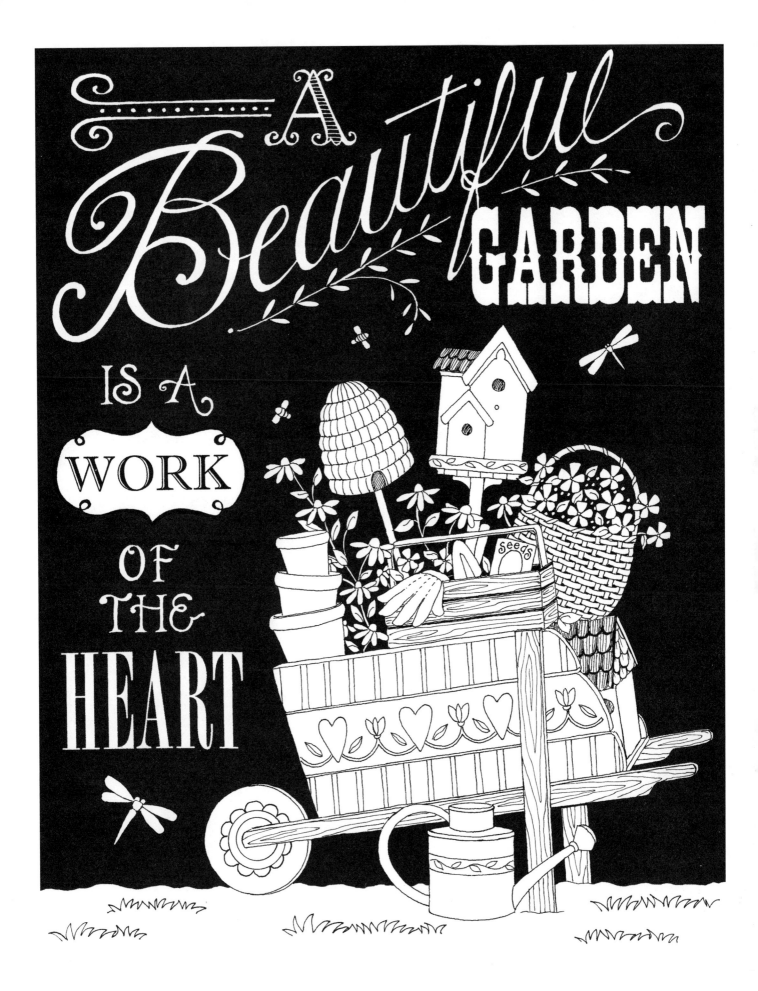

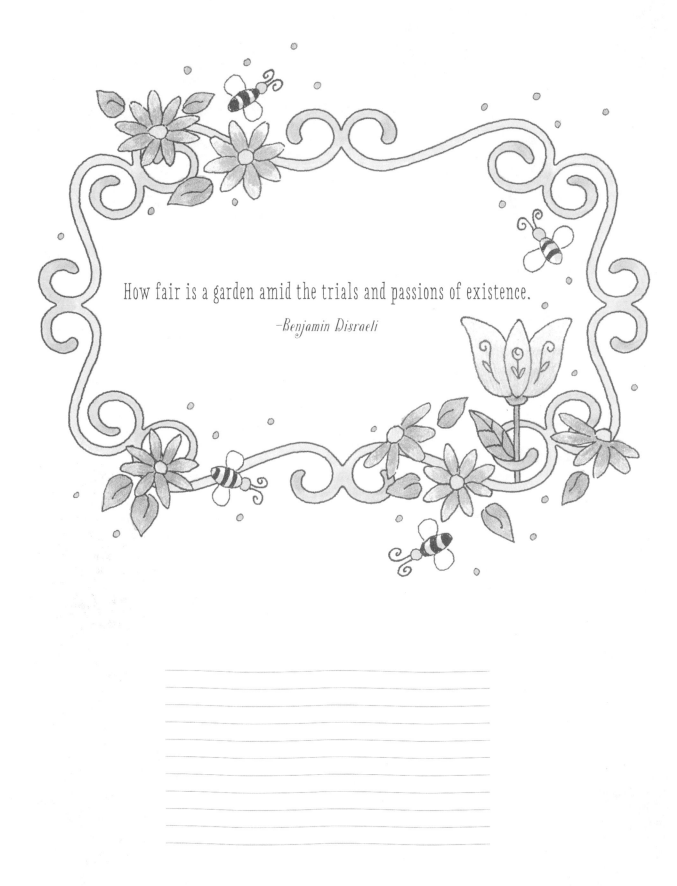

How fair is a garden amid the trials and passions of existence.

—Benjamin Disraeli

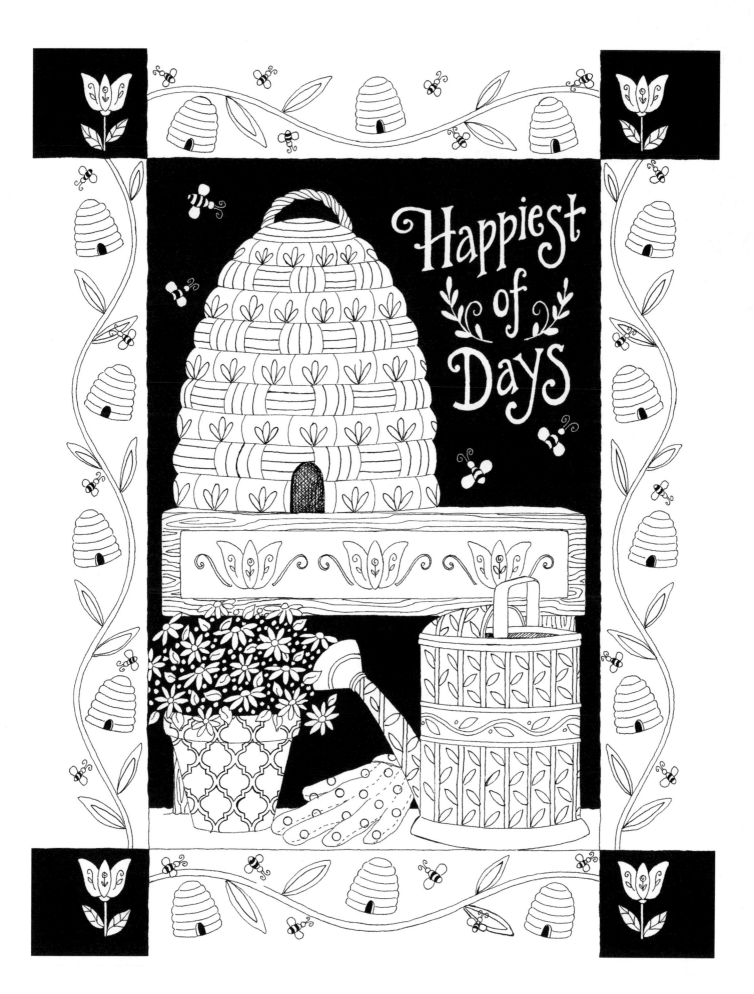

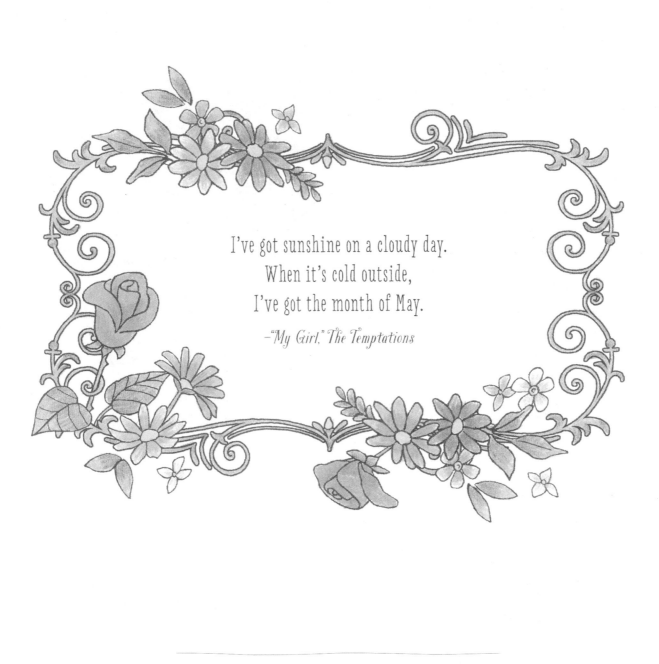

I've got sunshine on a cloudy day.
When it's cold outside,
I've got the month of May.

—"My Girl," The Temptations

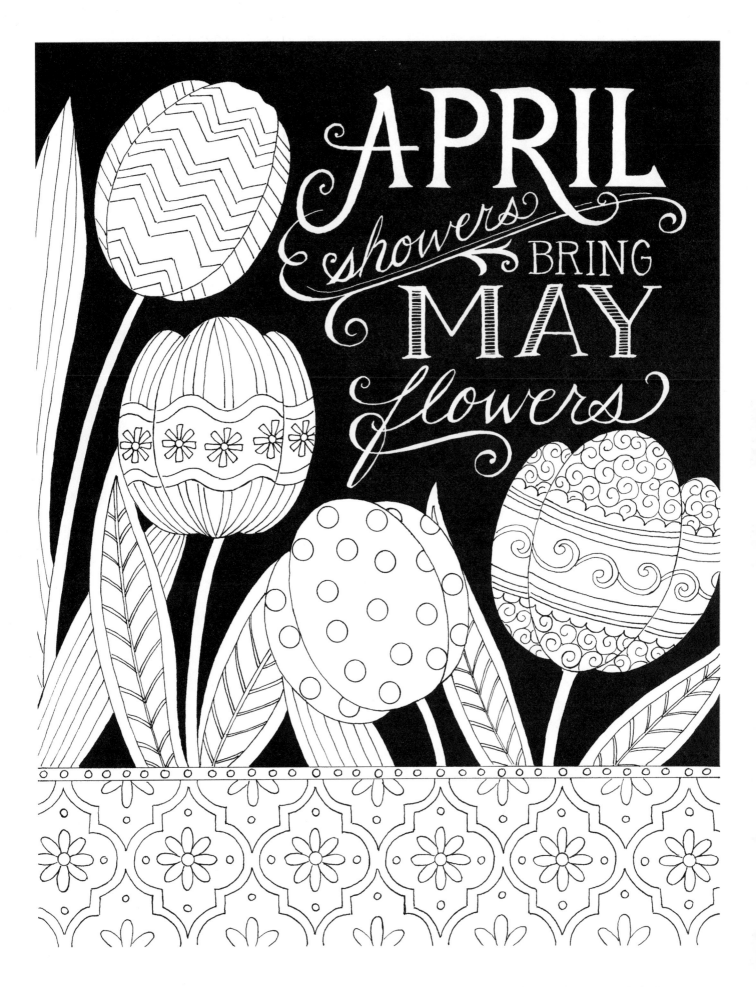

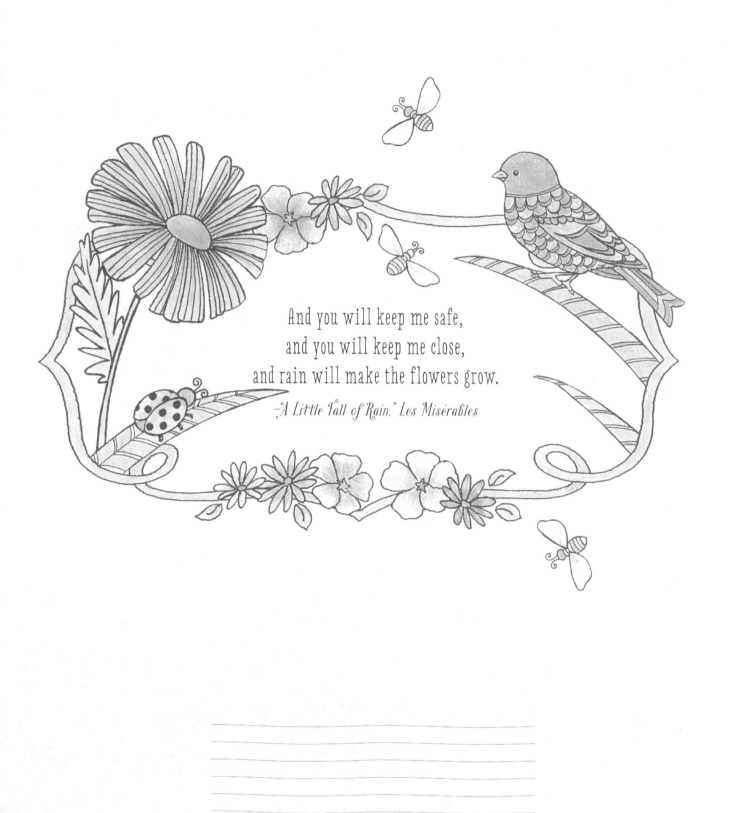

And you will keep me safe,
and you will keep me close,
and rain will make the flowers grow.

–"A Little Fall of Rain," Les Misérables

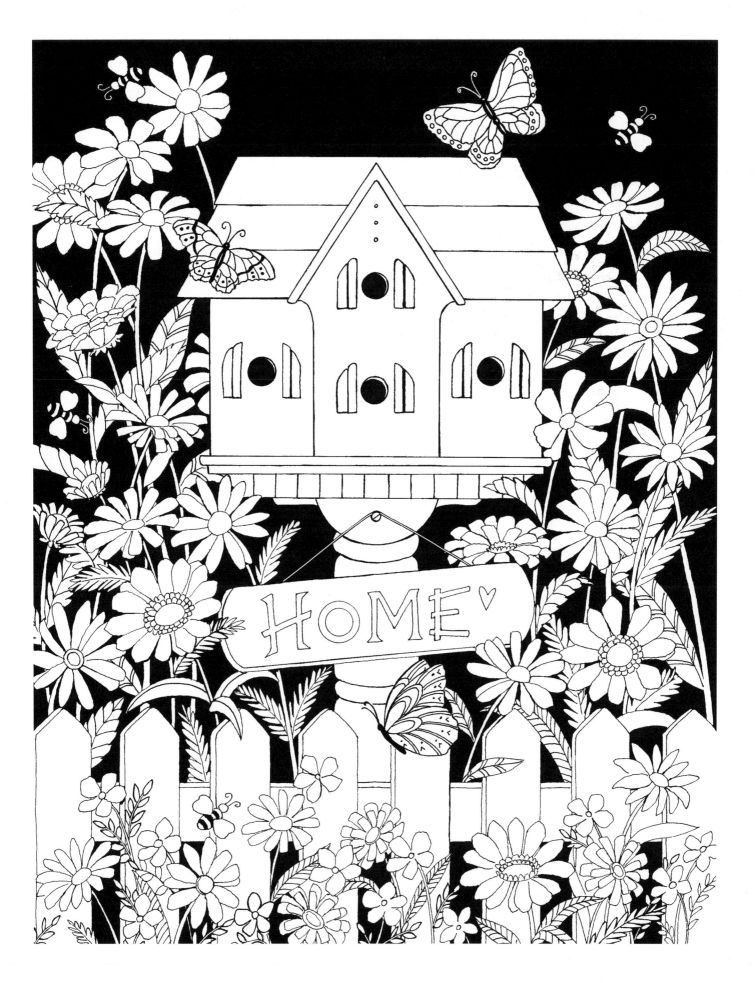

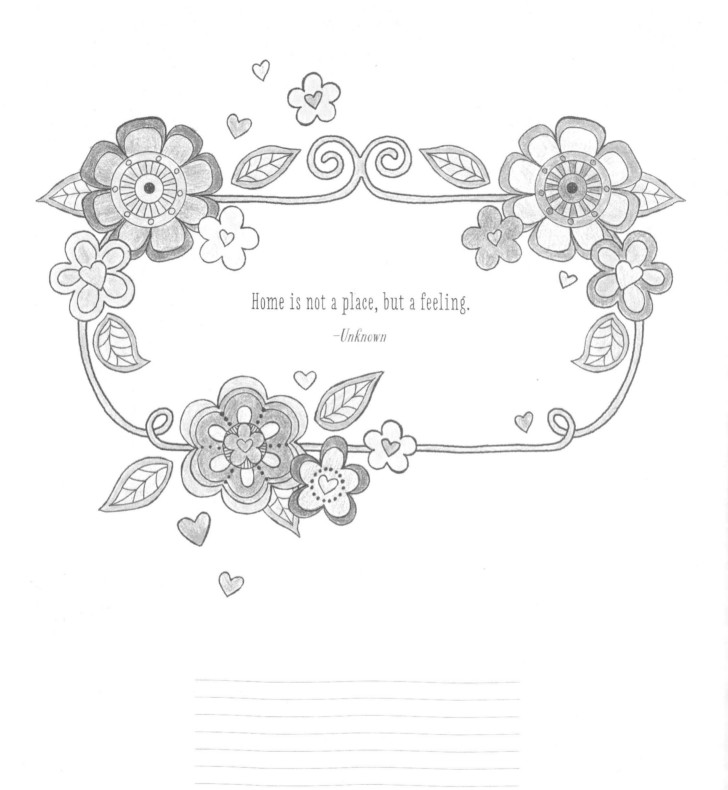

Home is not a place, but a feeling.

–Unknown

_____

_____

_____

_____

_____

_____

_____

_____

_____

_____